Date Due

Women's Career Development

Women's Career Development

Editors
Barbara A. Gutek and
Laurie Larwood

SAGE PUBLICATIONS
Newbury Park   Beverly Hills   London   New Delhi

For information address:

SAGE Publications, Inc.
2111 West Hillcrest Drive
Newbury Park, California 91320

SAGE Publications Inc.   SAGE Publications Ltd.
275 South Beverly Drive   28 Banner Street
Beverly Hills   London EC1Y 8QE
California 90212   England

SAGE PUBLICATIONS India Pvt. Ltd.
M-32 Market
Greater Kailash I
New Delhi 110 048 India

Printed in the United States of America

Library of Congress Cataloging-in-Publication Data

Main entry under title:

Women's career development.

Bibliography: p.
Includes index.
1. Women—Employment—United States. 2. Career development—United States. 3. Women—Employment—United States—Psychological aspects. I. Gutek, Barbara A. II. Larwood, Laurie.
HD6095.W698   1986   331.4'0973   86-6606
ISBN 0-8039-2717-7

Contents

1

Introduction
Women's Careers Are Important and Different

BARBARA A. GUTEK and LAURIE LARWOOD

This book contains a series of theoretical and empirical chapters that, taken together, describe important aspects of the careers of women. Each takes a different perspective, analyzes different groups of women, considers different points in time in the career process, and provides different comparisons—sometimes men, sometimes other groups of women. We have invited the essays featured here *because* of rather than despite their diversity. Our intention is to showcase some of the valuable, new, and different directions accomplished researchers are taking in examining the field of women's career development because it is this creative new work that is most likely to add to our understanding of this field.

The subject of women's career development has become increasingly important as the percentage of the American labor force that is female has increased from 15.2% a century ago to 43% today (Larwood & Wood, 1977, p. 15). The proportion of women in the labor force increased from 32% in 1960 to 53% in 1983 (U.S. Department of Labor, 1983)—and the proportion is expected to increase further (Flaim & Fullerton, 1978)—while the percentage of men in the labor force has gradually declined (Blau & Ferber, 1985). Similar changes in the labor force—especially large increases in the number of employed women— have been reported in other countries (Davidson & Cooper, 1984; Gutek, Larwood, & Stromberg, 1986).

Although throughout this century and even before some women spent their whole adult lives in the labor force, American society comfortably believed that women were merely casual workers who entered the work force only until they married and had children. Conveniently, employers offered women jobs that were easy to enter and that required relatively little training and afforded little potential for advancement. Thus there was little reason to study the career development of women. It was easily summarized: There was none. Men had careers; women had temporary employment or jobs that took second place to family interests and obligations. Researchers often agreed tacitly with this assessment by studying men's occupations and sometimes focusing on men's careers or employment experiences but passed up the opportunity to study women's experiences at work (see Gurin, Veroff, & Feld, 1960).

WHAT IS A CAREER?

The study of careers has changed rather dramatically over the past 20 years, reflecting some larger changes within psychology. At one time, consistent with views of human development, the young male adult was expected to choose a career once he had resolved whatever adolescent identity crisis he had. Once having chosen a career, the vocationally mature young man stuck with it.

Women were not necessarily expected to choose a career in the same way. Most women were expected to choose homemaking as a career, but they could not make concrete plans until they knew whom they would marry. Bardwick and Douvan (1972) argued that it is adaptive for women to remain flexible in their career plans if they wish to marry. Many women took jobs expecting that they would hold them only until they married or until they had children. They and their employers had similar expectations: they did not expect to advance in their work, and their employers expected them to leave.

Although they were in the minority, some women did choose a nontraditional occupation, and these women were the subject of intense scrutiny by researchers. First, they were assumed to be inferior in some way, frustrated and dissatisfied. Several researchers (Angrist & Almquist, 1975; Lewis, 1968) helped to debunk the notion that women who selected nontraditional careers were deviant, frustrated, or dissatisfied. Researchers then turned their attention to these nontraditional women—career pioneers or role innovators (Tangri, 1972)—who they were and why they selected nontraditional careers (see Nieva & Gutek, 1981, chap. 2, for a review of the literature).

Throughout the 1960s and early 1970s the conception of career fit with the prevailing notion of human development, emphasizing rapid change and development throughout childhood and adolescence and relative stability and lack of change in adulthood. The notion of developing one's career is relatively recent (see Hall, 1976) and is no doubt influenced by changes in views of adult development. Adulthood is not the static period that psychologists earlier envisioned; it is now viewed as a time of change and development.

Careers too are viewed as changing and developing. The very definition of career now encompasses the whole adult life cycle. For example, Hall (1976, p. 4) defined a career as an "individually perceived sequence of attitudes and behaviors associated with work-related experiences and activities over the span of the person's life." Thus a career can include a series of related jobs within an organization or different jobs within various companies. This series of positions represents the development of the career. As Schein (1978, p. 2) noted, "The essence of the career development perspective is the focus on the interaction of the individual and the organization over time" (see also London & Stumpf, 1982; Morgan, 1980). The notion of career development implies that the series of jobs represents some progress— for example, up the hierarchy, an increasingly large salary, increasing recognition and respect from one's colleagues, or more freedom to pursue one's own interest or select one's projects. The more one's career progresses in these ways, the more it is judged successful.

DIFFERENCES BETWEEN MEN AND WOMEN IN CAREER DEVELOPMENT

Both in the older emphasis on choice of career and the newer emphasis on career development, men—especially college-educated white men—have served as standards by which others, including women, were compared. Women are often studied to see how they depart from the male standard, both in choice of a career and in career development. As more and more women enter the labor force, some theorists suggest that women will behave more and more like men in the development of their careers. We, however, believe that women's careers are different and are likely to remain different in the near future for at least four reasons:

(1) There are differential expectations for men and women regarding the appropriateness of jobs for each sex that affect the kinds of jobs young men and women prepare for and select.

(2) Husbands and wives are differentially willing to accommodate themselves to each other's careers, with wives generally more willing to move or otherwise adapt to a husband's career needs than vice versa. To the extent that husbands receive more attractive job offers and their careers progress faster, this is a generally rational strategy to maximize total family career progress (see Markham, 1986; Pleck, 1977; Wallston, Foster, & Berger, 1978).

(3) The parent role is differentially defined for men and women; the mother role requires substantially more time and effort than the father role (Gutek et al., 1986).

(4) Compared to men, women are faced with more constraints in the workplace, including discrimination and various stereotypes detrimental to career advancement (see Larwood & Gutek, 1984).

RESEARCH ON
WOMEN'S CAREER DEVELOPMENT

Although women's careers are likely to be different from men's for some time, that does not mean that every study of women's career development should include a comparison with men. There are internal dynamics to women's careers that need to be examined, as several chapters in this volume will show. Theories about reference groups, relative deprivation, personality, and role conflict, among others, are used by various authors in this volume to study women's career development.

With the exception of the first and last essays, all of them are empirical. Rather than examine the attitudes or intentions of college students, the data presented in these chapters represent some form of field research—experimental, cross-section correlational, and longitudinal—showing real careers that are actually taking shape and the real problems encountered. The first provides a theoretical overview of some of the important thinking and issues concerning career development. Later chapters progress from issues of aspiration and reference groups through career paths to questions of family and career conflict. These are described briefly below.

Esther Diamond's "Theories of Career Development and the Reality of Women at Work" traces the evolution of theory concerning women's careers. As she points out, early thinking was based largely on the careers of men. Only recently have women become an issue and been regarded as the subject of separate theorizing. Diamond points out the need for more longitudinal research on careers and more theory dealing explicitly with women's careers.

The next chapter, by Mark Zanna, Faye Crosby, and George Loewenstein, "Male Reference Groups and Discontent Among Female Professionals," analyzes a sample of female professionals in an eastern city. How, the investigators asked, does the sex of one's reference group relate to the professional's situation? Women who compared themselves with men—a minority of women even in male dominated professions—differed in interesting ways from women whose reference groups consisted mostly of women.

Joanne Martin and her colleagues ("Now That I Can Have It, I'm Not So Sure I Want It") studied the reactions of secretaries who were shown slides depicting a firm in which women are employed in managerial ranks, or, alternatively, not so employed. The results of their experimental study are important for aspiration and deprivation theory development as well as for the consideration of careers. They conclude that a little success by some women in attaining managerial positions may depress the motivation of others rather than inspire them.

Susan Boardman, Charles Harrington, and Sandra Horowitz, in "Successful Women: A Psychological Investigation of Family Class and Education Origins," compared the psychological characteristics and life histories of two groups of successful women. Half of their sample might have been expected to succeed, judging from their socioeconomic backgrounds, whereas the others were "negative prediction defiers" who were not expected to achieve the career success they had attained. The sample of successful women shared many common characteristics, and both family background and race affected characteristics such as their reward orientation, locus of control, and relationship between personal and professional friendships.

Patricia Thomas's "Appraising the Performance of Women:

Gender and the Naval Officer" focuses on the Navy's efforts to provide an unbiased evaluation process for women officers. She notes that women are prevented from obtaining many Navy billets, and subsequently their experiences, which differ from men's, may result in differential performance evaluations and recommendations. After content analyzing the evaluations of officers who were candidates for promotion, she found that men and women were described differently—men as aggressive, mature, and logical; women as tactful. Composing a bogus description using these characteristics, she found that the characteristic male pattern was more likely to be recommended for promotion.

The next chapter, by Phyllis Bronstein, Leora Black, Joyce Pfennig, and Adele White, "Stepping onto the the Academic Career Ladder: How Are Women Doing?" turns attention to understanding how one acquires that crucial first job—in this case in academia. The curriculum vitae and letters of recommendation of applicants for academic positions were examined. In general, the findings are quite optimistic: Letters of reference are supportive and nonsexist. Men and women were equally qualified when length of time since Ph.D. was controlled. The authors did uncover some curious findings, however. In contrast to men, women apparently believed it was better to keep silent about family status. The only references to husbands and children were found on letters of recommendation for women, whereas men were more open about their family status. Despite the general lack of differences in presentation of job applicants, in a follow-up of participants in the study the authors found that men tended to find themselves in more prestigious jobs than women.

In their article, "A Comparison of the Career Paths Used by Successful Women and Men," Laurie Larwood and Urs Gattiker examine a sample of successful personnel in 17 corporations in California in order to trace the development of their careers. The results indicate that the success of younger men is less than that of older men, whereas the levels of hierarchical success for younger and older women are similar. Further, they point out that the careers of women are less predictable in leading from entry to advanced organizational positions. The results support hypotheses based on notions of career development, discrimination, and social change.

In the final empirical chapter, Roberta Valdez and Barbara Gutek, focusing on "Family Roles: A Help or a Hindrance for Working Women?" compare predictions of two competing theories in relation to family roles: role conflict and role accumulation. Using a representative sample of employed women in the Los Angeles area, they found that a larger than expected proportion of women in managerial positions is divorced or separated, supporting role conflict theory. In contrast, the highest levels of job satisfaction were found among the married, and the lowest level of job satisfaction was found among the never married, supporting role accumulation theory.

The last chapter by Laurie Larwood and Barbara Gutek, entitled "Working Toward a Theory of Women's Career Development," specifies some of the concepts that would be necessary to develop a theory of women's career development. They focus on five concerns: career preparation, the opportunities available in society, the influence of marriage, the influence of pregnancy and children, and timing and age. The authors show how these concepts can be used to specify a variety of career paths that women take. The mission of the chapter—indeed the whole book—is to stimulate additional research and theorizing on the topic of women's career development.

REFERENCES

Angrist, S. S., & Almquist, E. M. (1975). *Careers and contingencies.* New York: Dunellen.

Bardwick, J., & Douvan, E. (1972). Ambivalence: The socialization of women. In J. M. Bardwick (Ed.), *Readings on the psychology of women.* New York: Harper & Row.

Blau, F. D., & Ferber, M. A. (1985). Women in the labor market: The last twenty years. In L. Larwood, A. H. Stromberg, & B. A. Gutek (Eds.), *Women and work: An annual review* (Vol. 1). Beverly Hills, CA: Sage.

Davidson, M., & Cooper, C. (Eds.). (1984). *Women working: An international survey.* Chichester, England: John Wiley.

Flaim, P. O., & Fullerton, H. N. (1978). Labor force projections to 1990: Three possible paths. *Monthly Labor Review* (Dec.), 25-35.

Gurin, G., Veroff, J., & Feld, S. (1960). *Americans view their mental health.* New York: Basic Books.

Gutek, B. A., Larwood, L., & Stromberg, A. H. (1986). Women at work. In C. Cooper & I. Robertson (Eds.), *Review of industrial/organisational psychology* (Vol. 1). Chichester, England: John Wiley.

Hall, D. T. (1976). *Careers in organizations.* Santa Monica, CA: Goodyear.

Larwood, L., & Gutek, B. A. (1984). Women at work in the U.S. In M. Davidson & C. Cooper (Eds.), *Women working: An international survey.* Chichester, England: John Wiley.

Larwood, L., & Wood, M. M. (1977). *Women in management.* Lexington, MA: D. C. Heath.

Lewis, E. C. (1968). *Developing women's potential.* Ames: Iowa State University Press.

London, M., & Stumpf, S. A. (1982). *Managing careers.* Reading, MA: Addison-Wesley.

Markham, W. T. (1986). Sex, relocation, and occupational advancement: The "real cruncher" for women. In A. H. Stromberg, L. Larwood, & B. A. Gutek (Eds.), *Women and work: An annual review* (Vol. 2). Beverly Hills, CA: Sage.

Morgan, M. A. (Ed.). (1980). *Managing career development.* New York: D. Van Nostrand.

Nieva, V. F., & Gutek, B. A. (1981). *Women and work: A psychological perspective.* New York: Praeger.

Pleck, J. (1977). The work-family role system. *Social Problems, 24,* 417-427.

Schein, E. H. (1978). *Career dynamics: Matching individual and organizational needs.* Reading, MA: Addison-Wesley.

Tangri, S. (1972). Determinants of occupational role innovation among college women. *Journal of Social Issues, 28,* 177-199.

U.S. Department of Labor. (1983). *Time of change: 1983 Handbook on women workers* (Bulletin 298). Washington, DC: U.S. Department of Labor.

Wallston, B. S., Foster, M., & Berger, M. (1978). I will follow him: Myth, reality, or forced choice? *Psychology of Women Quarterly, 3,* 9-21.

2

Theories of Career Development and the Reality of Women at Work

ESTHER E. DIAMOND

Traditional career development theory was based almost exclusively on studies of male subjects and gave little attention to the fact that for women the development process over the life span was different from that of men and far more complex in terms of frequent shifts between home and work and the effects of their socialization on their attitudes, role expectations, and behaviors. Although several promising attempts have been made to provide one, little exists today in the way of a fully developed theory of women's career development. This chapter examines the various career development theories as they relate to women and to their current status in the world of work.

Until relatively recently little attention was paid to the career development of women as following a somewhat different pattern from and being somewhat more complex than that of men. (The term "career development" here, as in almost all of the pertinent literature, is used interchangeably with "vocational development" and includes career choice as part of the process.) Traditional career development theorists (for example, Super, 1957; Ginzberg, Ginsburg, Axelrad, & Herma, 1951) originally based their theories almost exclusively on studies of male subjects.

Gilligan (1979) argued that theories of the life cycle, by taking for their model the lives of men, have failed to account for the experience of women. "Implicitly adopting the male life as the norm, they (psychological theorists) have tried to fashion women out of a masculine cloth" (p. 432). Woman's place in man's life cycle, Gilligan stated further, "has been that of nurturer, caretaker, and helpmate, the weaver of those networks of relationships on which she in turn relies" (p. 440). Brooks (1984) expressed a similar point of view. Women, she contended, are socialized to give primacy to nurturing roles, and career or achieving roles assume secondary or negligible priority.

Gilligan and Brooks's descriptions of woman's role in man's life cycle is dramatically illustrated by the case of Mary Cunningham (1984). Relating the story of what really happened at Bendix, Cunningham said of an early decision not to leave her job as an executive although the tensions had begun to build: "Bill Agee [Chairman of the Board] told me he needed me, and that was all I needed to hear. Everything I'd been taught . . .—to stick close when the chips are down, to help, to endure—convinced me not to leave" (p. 24). But, she pointed out, when Agee was in a similar situation at another company he chose to leave for the sake of his career. She explained the difference between his behavior and hers as follows:

> Part of the problem, I think, is the different ways in which Bill and I—in which men and women—view their careers. Bill was interested in helping Hansberger [his mentor], no doubt, but up to a point. Always he kept an eye on his own career. I viewed serving Bill as an end in itself and mistakenly viewed this as the means to best further my career. . . . Women, for whatever reasons, biological or cultural, have learned to act as nurturers. The emphasis for us has been more on people. For men, the emphasis has been more on careers (p. 26).

HOW THEORIES OF
CAREER DEVELOPMENT REGARD WOMEN

Brown (1984), reviewing the literature on occupational choice, found that not until 1975 did women's career development, in the currently accepted view as a lifelong process, begin to be studied extensively. A review of the literature published in 1970, Brown found, included only a handful of studies with women as subjects. Early career development theorists such as Super, Ginzberg, and Krumbolz gave primacy to women's homemaker role; and even though in later years they tried to take into account gender and other sociocultural demographic variables, none has yet developed propositions that specify the effects of these variables (Brooks, 1984).

Ginzberg (Ginzberg et al., 1951; Ginzberg, 1972, 1984; also see Brown, 1984) chose as the basic sample for his initial study upper-income males from Protestant or Catholic backgrounds. He added two additional groups: high school males from low-income families and ten college women—seven Barnard sophomores and three Barnard seniors. No high school females were included. Among the women—hardly a representative group—he found the career development process not markedly different from that of males, except that concerns about marriage became more important in their planning as they neared the end of their undergraduate studies. He thought he could distinguish three groups: marriage-oriented, work-oriented, and women hoping to combine both.

For women, Ginzberg found, the tentative period of career development corresponded closely to the same period for men, occurring at approximately ages 11 to 18 and consisting of four stages—interests, capacity, value, and transition to the reality period. Following the capacity stage, however, in which the congruence between one's interests and one's capacities begins to be considered, gender differences began to be apparent. By the transition stage the women were heavily oriented toward marriage. Of course, many men are also oriented toward marriage as they complete their schooling, but for them traditionally there has been no conflict between marriage and career. In the 1970s Ginzberg (1972) concluded that the male model of career preparation and choice did not fit the female prototype—that many women interrupted their educational preparation for marriage and experienced frequent shifts between home and work.

Super's theory of vocational development (1957, 1984), which he defines as implementation of one's self-concept, integrates a number of variables that influence the development of a self-concept throughout the individual's life span. These include biological, societal, and psychological variables. Career patterns of men, according to Super, are essentially applicable to women if modified to take marriage and childbearing into account. He described patterns for women as "stable homemaking, conventional (working followed by marriage), stable working, double-track (working while homemaking), interrupted (working, homemaking, and working, either while homemaking or after having given up homemaking), unstable, and multiple-trial" (1984, pp. 215-216). Patterns found for men, on the other hand, were stable, conventional, unstable, and multiple-trial. Super also hypothesized that in theory there is no difference in the part self-concept plays in male and female career development: Both "appear to make decisions on the basis of their self-concepts and their concepts of the circumstances in which they live" (1984, p. 216).

In Holland's view (1966), vocational choice is perceived as an expression of personality, reflecting also the individual's motivation, knowledge, and ability. Occupations are seen as a way of life, "an environment rather than a set of isolated work functions or skills" (p. 4). Vocational satisfaction depends on the congruence between personality and working environment. Holland's theory explains existing phenomena—things as they are today, regardless of underlying sociological processes or causes. On his Self-Directed Search (SDS), a vocational interest inventory yielding scores on the six dimensions of his theoretical model, men generally get Realistic/Investigative/Enterprising (RIE) codes, whereas women obtain Social/Artistic/Conventional (SAC) codes—results that have brought accusations of sexism (Weinrach, 1984). Women who have spent most of their time raising children, as opposed to working outside the home, generally have a summary code of Social/Artistic/Enterprising (SAE). Holland argues that no one escapes his or her life history, which makes the individual suited for some groups of occupations and not for others (Holland, 1975). In Holland's schema, personality tends to be viewed as somewhat static, unchanging, which implies that women are not likly to change insofar as career orientation, interests, and goals are concerned and which ignores the catalytic role that various kinds of career development intervention might play. Moreover, this view is likely to perpetuate the status quo and to support self-fulfilling prophecies regarding women in the world of work.

TOWARD A NEW THEORY OF
WOMEN'S CAREER DEVELOPMENT?

Is a separate theory of women's career development needed? Expert opinion is divided. Osipow (1983) noted that although there are some similarities between the sexes in the career development process, there are enough differences to warrant attempts to develop distinctive theories for each, "at least until such time as true sexual equality of career opportunity exists and the results have permeated society at all levels" (p. 263).

Fitzgerald and Crites (1980) expressed the belief that the major career development theories provide some useful concepts for counseling women and that the career development process for women is not essentially different from that for men. They observed, however, that it is more complex for women because of the differences in socialization and in the combination of attitudes, role expectations, behaviors, and sanctions that constitute it. Women, they contended, will not achieve equity with men until they have similar access to financial resources and are not dependent on others for their livelihood.

Brooks (1984) observed that the socialization of women to give primacy to nurturing roles and secondary or negligible priority to career or achieving roles leads to home-career conflict, lack of serious career planning, restriction of options to sex-stereotypical occupations, and the occurrence of such external variables as discrimination in the workplace. She cited Laws's observation that women's view of life after 30 lacks a crystallized pattern for living: Women plan for marriage but not divorce or widowhood, and they plan for children but not for children's growing up and leaving the "nest." Nor do they consider the fact that most women will spend a third of their adult lives alone.

Richardson (1974) asserted that although the vocational decisions boys and girls are faced with in school appear to be similar, the meaning of those decisions becomes increasingly divergent with age as women progress through adolescence and young adulthood. Further, "although young women no longer see marriage and family responsibilities as excluding involvement in an occupation, the two aspects of female role development exist in somewhat uneasy alliance" (p. 136). Moreover, Richardson pointed out, the parameters of existing vocational maturity models are "the life stages [e.g., exploration and establishment] and coping behaviors involved in the development of a career role in the occupational world, a process of development which is more continuous for men than for women" (p. 137). A model of vocational maturity and career development that would fit women would need to attach more importance to exploration of and establishment in the traditional roles of wife and mother.

Richardson (1974) described three modal career patterns with reference to women: a continuous uninterrupted work pattern, characteristic of women who may not marry or who delay marriage or childbearing until they have established themselves in an occupation; work-oriented women, who place equal priority on both aspects of their role development, dropping out of the work force for limited periods of time but working more or less continuously in the labor force; and homemaking women, who place high priority on traditional role development and have little concern for exploration and establishment in the occupational world.

Astin (1984), asked to prepare a "comprehensive yet parsimonious theoretical statement" (p. 117) on the career development of women, proposed a model of career development that, she suggests, can be used to explain the occupational behavior of both men and women. Her premise is that "basic work motivation is the same for men and women, but that they make different choices because their early socialization experiences and structural opportunities are different" (p. 118). She describes the model as a sociopsychological model that incorporates the influence of the social context on the individual and his or her work behavior, which she regards as a social behavior. The model incorporates four major constructs: motivation, work expectations, sex-role socialization, and the structure of opportunity. It places a great deal of emphasis on the changing structure of opportunity—the way in which social forces shape and reshape occupational decisions—and its impact on contemporary women and their occupational behavior.

Astin's model has been hailed as a fresh, new, and provocative contribution by a number of individuals prominent in the field of women's career development (e.g., Farmer, 1984). Others, however, including some who agree that the work is important in opening up new theoretical aspects for consideration, are somewhat more critical of the model's shortcomings, citing poorly defined constructs and the need for more conceptual and empirical work (e.g., Fitzgerald & Betz, 1984; Harmon, 1984). Perhaps one of the most substantive responses to Astin's model was that of Gilbert (1984), who questioned whether it sufficiently addressed the realities of the career development of women—specifically the schism between our current institutional structure and the demands of family roles. Even when men and women make the required changes in traditional sex-role beliefs and behavior and expect a career to include active participation in both occupational and family roles, the problem of societal structure still arises. She points to a study of women scientists hampered in their efforts to combine family life with a career in the sciences by the common belief among male scientists that in order to be successful they need to work 90 hours a week. She asks, "Can a concept of career that includes involvement in family and occupational roles (and principles of equity between men and women) realistically co-exist with social institutions that embody the values of a patriarchal society?" (p. 129).

Nieva and Gutek (1981) carefully distinguished between women's career *choices* (defined as preferences) and the jobs or occupations they finally work at. Personality variables influence the former, the authors asserted, and the process is mainly psychological. The latter, however, is influenced by a number of demographic variables and economic considerations—pay, convenience, home responsibilities, husband's attitude, availability, and so on—somewhat akin to Astin's (1984) structure of opportunity. The process of linking up with an occupation, they pointed out, is a reciprocal one, although the literature makes it appear to be "a one-way process . . . with women doing all the deciding" (p. 9), whereas organizations also select. The authors' literature search also strengthened the suggestion that there are at least three groups of women with reference to career commitment: committed to nontraditional careers, committed to traditional careers, and committed to the homemaker role.

Perun and Bielby (1981) took the position that "a solution to the current theoretical morass will be found only when women's occupational behavior is viewed from the human development paradigm which emphasizes process, comprehensiveness, and a life course perspective" (p. 248). Recognition that social structure and social change profoundly affect women's occupational behavior is intrinsic to the paradigm. The authors reject the assumption of existing theories that vocational choice is a function of interindividual differences; this, they maintain, is not true in the case of women.

SOME THINGS ARE CHANGING . . .

How will the changing picture of women in the working world today affect the process of their career development? Although there have been some changes in the occupational distribution of men and women, women are still concentrated in low-paying deadend jobs, according to a report on women workers by the U.S. Department of Labor (1983). Of all employed women, 55% are in two occupational groups: clerical, which is the largest single category, and service work, which includes food handlers, health service workers, personal service workers, and the like. Nevertheless, the report states, legislation of the 1960s and 1970s has had some effect on the occupational distribution of women, and by the end of the 1970s they had begun to move into the skilled crafts, managerial positions, and other jobs traditionally held by men, with women under 35 making the greatest inroads into male-dominated occupational domains. The differences in occupational distribution, however, are still sizable. For example, although the proportion employed in professional and technical jobs is roughly the same for both sexes, women are more likely to be employed in traditional female jobs such as nurse, health technologist, or technician; elementary or secondary school teacher; librarian; and social worker. Men, on the other hand, are more likely to be engineers, architects, lawyers and judges, and physicians, dentists, and related practitioners. Men are also three times more likely than women to work in blue-collars jobs. In 1981, 21% of all employed men, but only 2% of employed women, were craft and kindred workers (although the number of women craft workers increased from 391,000 to 803,000 between 1972 and 1981).

As for combining home and career, the Bureau of Labor Statistics reported that women either are not leaving their jobs following childbirth or are returning to them shortly afterward. Between 1973 and 1983 the participation rate in the labor force for mothers with children under age 3 rose from 30% to 46% (U.S. Department of Labor, 1984).

Osipow (1983) cited changes in the proportions of women in various nontraditional occupations over the past two to three decades as evidence that sex-stereotyped attitudes toward work and work roles are not impervious to change. He cited several studies, including a cross-sectional comparison of women at three educational levels, that indicated that desire for marriage was an important career variable at the junior high school level and an important aspect of planning by the time women reached college. Plans at all three levels included a combination of work, marriage, and family responsibilities. He interpreted the frequency of choice of sex-stereotyped occupations as possible motivation for smoothly combining home and career.

... WHILE OTHERS REMAIN THE SAME

A variety of attitudes and behaviors still set up barriers to women's optimal career development, and particularly to their participation in nontraditional occupations. In vocational education programs, for example, despite the protection of Title IX of the Education Amendments of 1972, traditional attitudes about the appropriate vocational role for women often predominate, discouraging entry into nontraditional training and resulting in harassment of those who do enter (Farmer & Sidney, 1985). Hostile behavior toward women in nontraditional jobs is illustrated dramatically by a story in *Civil Rights Update* ("Woman Trucker," 1980). A women trucker was fired "for her own good" after release from a hospital following a beating and rape near her disabled vehicle. Company mechanics had refused to repair the vehicle.

Working women who become pregnant also are often victims of diehard stereotypical attitudes (Adams, 1984). They may find themselves removed from the fast track, excluded from important meetings, and in general reduced to a lesser role. High-achieving women, Adams reported, have very high expectations in both home and career areas and have to seek out companies and professions that will accommodate family life. They may have to avoid jobs in sales, marketing, or other work involving extensive travel. These findings are clearly related to Gilbert's (1984) observation regarding the schism between family roles and current institutional structures.

Carlson (1984), writing about the development of women as middle managers, described the Smith College Management Program, established for women only. She cited Susan C. Lowance, the program's director, who had found that in management programs at Dartmouth, Stanford, Harvard, and the Massachusetts Institute of Technology women constituted only about 6% of the students.

Whiteside and Mosier ("Devoted Woman," 1984) surveyed about 1500 women and men who had received MBAs from the University of Texas over a 60-year period. Women workaholics, they found, reaped fewer rewards than their male counterparts and were more likely than men to be single or divorced or married several times: 52% of the women but only 17% of the men were single.

The workplace and the educational institutions are not the only places where stereotyped attitudes toward women's roles are putting up a tough last-ditch battle. Studies reported at an American Psychological Association convention indicated that even if their wives work, most men do no more than one-third of the household tasks (Cunningham, 1983). Many men see participation in "feminine" household tasks and child-rearing as a threat to their masculinity and undergo attitude change only when faced with a crisis such as a wife's illness, death, or desertion, when they must assume full responsibility for the household.

Similar findings were reported in a nationwide study of money, work, and sex among more than 3600 married couples and 653 cohabiting couples, as well as gay and Lesbian couples (Blumstein & Schwartz, 1983). In-depth interviews and questionnaires were followed up 18 months later. The investigators found that although wives working outside the home did less housework than homemakers, they still did most of the housework. Among middle- and upper-class couples, wives did more housework than their husbands, but they were able to shift some of the burden to hired household help. Working-class husbands, however, did little housework, expressing the opinion that it was rightfully their wives' domain. Cohabiting (unmarried) couples set more egalitarian standards, but the women who worked outside the home full-time still wound up doing more of the housework than their partners; often earned income of each of the partners served as a basis for assigning household duties. For both married and cohabiting couples, men's aversion to housework was a serious source of conflict—more so among the former than the latter. The investigators also found that "men tend to judge people, including their partners, by what they accomplish in the work world. They evaluate the importance of a person's time by its market value" (p. 151).

Rix and Stone (1984) pointed out that "As long as it is women who are the ones to step off the fast track to meet family responsibilities, they will be at a competitive disadvantage in career advancement as it is presently structured" (p. 210). They cited Census Bureau and other data that indicate that family responsibilities cause working mothers to make decisions that limit their opportunities for good jobs and advancement—especially in the case of managerial women with young children who are competing with male colleagues for higher-level jobs. The problem, the authors assert, is that "the years during which women who want children must bear and raise them are the key years in the struggle for career success" (p. 212); the corporate or professional structure does not adapt its policies to accommodate the pressures that working mothers face. The structure is based, rather, on "what could be expected of male employees whose traditional-role marriages allowed fathers consistently to resolve work/family conflicts in favor of the job" (p. 212).

Finally, continuing stereotypical attitudes were exemplified by an advertisement for *Newsweek* magazine during the 1984 presidential campaign. The advertisement featured a large photograph of Geraldine Ferraro and the words "Mondale's right-hand man. It's a woman." The implication appeared to be that only by being a man or as much like one as possible can a woman fulfill traditionally male roles.

A CONCLUDING NOTE

A clear picture of the career development process for women has not yet emerged, and it may well be premature to formulate a theory that explains it, as it has been little more than a decade since dramatic changes in women's role in the working world began to take place. Given that career development is viewed as a lifelong process, involving such aspects of one's development as self-concept, interests, values, all levels of decision-making and choices, and exploration and evaluation of educational, work, and leisure opportunities, much more research is obviously needed. There is a particular need for longitudinal studies, following up an adequate sample of women, including working-class women, from their early years through high school, post-high school education, and as far into their working years as possible. Such research must not be based on the male model but must be relevant to the many unique aspects of women's experience and involve broad enough samples of women to embrace all the pertinent variables—socioeconomic, demographic, educational, environmental, biological, and psychological. Astin's (1984) model and some of the suggestions made by the respondents to the model should be tested empirically and longitudinally. Only then can the process of career development for women, and its similarities to and differences from the career development process for men, be more fully understood.

REFERENCES

Adams, J. M. (1984, February 20). When working women become pregnant. *New England Business*, pp. 18-21.

Astin, H. S. (1984). The meaning of work in women's lives: A sociopsychological model of career choice and work behavior. *The Counseling Psychologist, 12*, 117-126.

Blumstein, P., & Schwartz, P. (1983). *American couples: Money, work, sex*. New York: William Morrow.

Brooks, L. (1984). Counseling special groups: Women and ethnic minorities. In D. Brown, L. Brooks, & Associates (Eds.), *Career choice and development* (pp. 355-368). San Francisco: Jossey-Bass.

Brown, D. (1984). Summary, comparison, and critique of major theories. In D. Brown, L. Brooks, & Associates (Eds.), *Career choice and development* (pp. 311-336). San Francisco: Jossey-Bass.

Carlson, B. (1984, February 20). Developing women as middle managers with Smith course. *New England Business*, pp. 19-20.

Cunningham, M. (1984, July). What really happened at Bendix. *United*, pp. 23-24, 26, 154-159, 162, 164, 166.

Cunningham, S. (1983, November). Women still do a majority of child care, housework. *APA Monitor*, p. 16.

Devoted woman worker loses out. (1984, July 23). *Seattle Post-Intelligencer*, Section C, page 1.

Farmer, H. S. (1984). A shiny fresh minted penny. *The Counseling Psychologist, 12*, 141-144.

Farmer, H. S., & Sidney, J. S. (1984). Sex equity in career and vocational education. In S. Klein (Ed.), *Handbook for achieving sex equity through education* (pp. 338-359). Baltimore, MD: Johns Hopkins University Press.

Fitzgerald, L. F., & Betz, N. E. (1984). Astin's model: A technical and philosophical critique. *The Counseling Psychologist, 12*, 135-138.

Fitzgerald, L. F., & Crites, J. O. (1980). Toward a career psychology of women: What do we know? What do we need to know? *Journal of Counseling Psychology, 27*, 44-62.

Gilbert, L. A. (1984). Comments on the meaning of work in women's lives. *The Counseling Psychologist, 12*, 129-130.

Gilligan, C. (1979). Woman's place in man's life cycle. *Harvard Educational Review, 49*, 431-446.

Ginzberg, E. (1972). Toward a theory of occupational choice: A restatement. *Vocational Guidance Quarterly, 20*, 169-176.

Ginzberg, E. (1984). Career development. In D. Brown, L. Brooks, & Associates (Eds.), *Career choice and development* (pp. 169-191). San Francisco: Jossey-Bass.

Ginzberg, E., Ginsburg, S. W., Axelrad, S., & Herma, J. L. (1951). *Occupational choice: An approach to a general theory*. New York: Columbia University Press.

Harmon, L. W. (1984). What's new? A response to Astin. *The Counseling Psychologist, 12*, 127-128.

Holland, J. L. (1966). *The psychology of vocational choice*. Waltham, MA: Blaisdell.

Holland, J. L. (1975). The use and evaluation of interest inventories and simulations. In E. E. Diamond (Ed.), *Issues of sex bias and sex fairness in career interest measurement* (pp. 19-44). Washington, DC: National Institute of Education.

Nieva, V. F., & Gutek, B. A. (1981). *Women and work: A psychological perspective.* New York: Praeger.

Osipow, S. H. (1983). *Theories of career development.* Englewood Cliffs, NJ: Prentice-Hall.

Perun, P. J., & Belby, D.D.V. (1981). Towards a model of female occupational behavior: A human development approach. *Psychology of Women Quarterly, 6,* 234-252.

Richardson, M. S. (1974). Vocational maturity in counseling girls and women. In D. E. Super (Ed.), *Measuring vocational maturity for counseling and evaluation* (pp. 135-144). Washington, DC: National Vocational Guidance Association.

Rix, S. E., & Stone, A. J. (1984). Work. In S. M. Pritchard, *The women's annual* (No. 4). Boston: G. K. Hall.

Super, D. E. (1957). *The psychology of careers.* New York: Harper.

Super, D. E. (1984). Career and life development. In D. Brown, L. Brooks, & Associates (Eds.), *Career choice and development* (pp. 192-234). San Francisco: Jossey-Bass.

U.S. Department of Labor (1983). *Time of change: 1983 handbook on women workers.* Women's Bureau Bulletin 298. Washington, DC: U.S. Government Printing Office.

U.S. Department of Labor, Bureau of Labor Statistics (1984). *Employment in perspective: Working women.* Report 712. Washington, DC: Author.

Weinrach, S. G. (1984). Determinants of vocational choice: Holland's theory. In D. Brown, L. Brooks, & Associates (Eds.), *Career choice and development* (pp. 61-93). San Francisco: Jossey-Bass.

Woman Trucker (1980, February). *Civil Rights Update,* p. 2.

3

Male Reference Groups and Discontent Among Female Professionals

MARK P. ZANNA, FAYE CROSBY, and GEORGE LOEWENSTEIN

A sample of employed women in Newton, Massachusetts, was used to test an aspect of relative deprivation theory: Will women who have a male reference group experience greater deprivation, resentment, or grievance at work than women who have a female reference group? The data show that although relatively few women have a male reference group, they do exhibit less satisfaction and more deprivation. They also differ from other women in significant ways, such as family status (most were married, childless women) and income (higher than incomes of women with a female reference group).

The North American labor market has traditionally been segregated by gender. Men and women have worked in different and disparate occupations. More often than not they have also worked in locations that are physically separated. Women have, in the words of L. K. Howe (1977), been encapsulated in "pink-collar ghettos."

Recently researchers have wondered what happens when women enter the paid labor market in large numbers and perhaps even

Authors' Note: We wish to thank the editors, along with Mel Lerner, James Olson, and Betsy Zanna, for comments on earlier versions of this chapter.

become integrated into occupations that have traditionally been reserved for males. What happens as more and more North American women have careers and not just jobs? Will women in high-prestige occupations compare themselves to men? If so, will they feel upset, even angry, about the comparison?

These and similar questions concerning career development were at the heart of a survey conducted during 1978 and 1979 in Newton, Massachusetts. The main point of the survey was to test the theory of relative deprivation and to apply it to the paradox of the contented female worker (Crosby, 1982). The theory of relative deprivation, in brief, states that feelings of deprivation, resentment, or grievance (which are taken to be synonyms) do not vary simply as a function of one's objective condition but depend, instead, on how the objective conditions compare to certain psychological standards. Ever since Stouffer and his colleagues first coined the term "relative deprivation" (Stouffer, Suchman, DeVinney, Star, & Williams, 1949), researchers and theorists have linked the concept of relative deprivation to the concepts of reference group (Merton & Rossi, 1957) and "comparison other" (see Suls & Miller, 1977). The survey included not only measures of grievance but also measures of all of the factors—including one's referents or comparisons—that various theorists (e.g., Gurr, 1970; Runciman, 1966) have identified as contributing to feelings of grievance.

Included in the survey's sample were 163 employed women, 182 employed men, and 90 housewives. All of the respondents were white and between the ages of 25 and 40. All had resided in Newton at least a year prior to being interviewed. Half of the employed people worked in high-status occupations: lawyers, physicians, professors, and so on. The other half worked in low-status jobs such as clerks or waitresses. Half of the housewives' husbands had high-status occupations whereas half were in low-status jobs.

Questions on the survey instrument asked people's attitudes on three main topics: one's own job (if employed), the job situation of women in the United States, and one's own domestic situation. For each topic respondents were asked a number of questions about their feelings of deprivation and about whether they believed they were obtaining what they wanted, what they deserved, what they thought others had, and what they had expected to obtain. They were also asked about their views of the future and about any feelings they had that they were to blame for the failure to obtain all they wanted.

A major finding of the Newton survey (see Crosby, 1982) was that the employed women, like the employed women in earlier surveys, felt contented with their own jobs. Their contentment was all the more striking because there was strong evidence that the women in the sample were, in fact, victims of sex discrimination: They earned per annum nearly $8,000 less (on average) than did the men in the sample who were exactly comparable to the women on all of the measured variables relevant to salary (e.g., years of training). Furthermore, the employed women, even more than the employed men and the housewives in the sample, were aware of sex discrimination in general and felt aggrieved about it.

Why, then, did the employed women in Newton remain blind to their own disadvantage? One possible reason that they thought they were obtaining what they wanted and deserved to obtain from their jobs was that they used a restricted reference group for comparison. Most of the respondents in the survey named another person of the same gender when asked to whom they compared themselves in deciding how good their own jobs were. As Figure 3.1 shows, the only group to break this trend at all was the group of women with high-prestige jobs. Fully 60% of the time even these women, whom we can label professional or career women, named another woman as the "comparison person."

The present chapter looks more closely at the career women in the Newton survey and their reference groups. We ask three sets of questions. First, among the women with high-prestige jobs (40% of whom selected a male as their first comparison person), are there any who have a male reference group? That is, do some of the women use males exclusively or predominantly as their referents for determining how good their own jobs are? The interviewer actually asked each survey participant to name up to three people used for comparative purposes; and so the first question is: Do any of the women name three men? Second, if there are any women with a male reference group, who are they? What are their demographic characteristics? Are they, for example, more likely to be single or more likely to be married? Finally, and most important, what distinctive attitudes do they hold? Do women with a male reference group feel more, or less, angry than other women about their jobs and/or the job situation of women in general?

Although relative deprivation theory does not allow us to predict whether there are women who have a male reference group (let alone

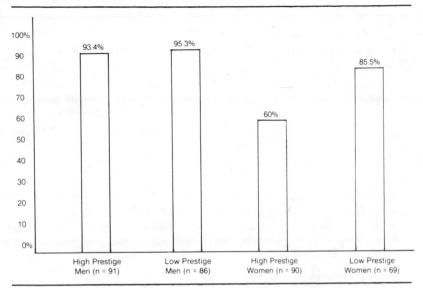

Figure 3.1. Percentages naming, as first choice, a person of their own gender in response to the question, "In trying to decide how good your own job is, do you ever compare yourself with anyone else?" Adapted from Crosby (1982).

what their demographic characteristics might be), it does suggest that if we are ever to discover a group of women who feel deprived in their jobs, it will be those women who socially compare themselves with otherwise similar men and who are, as a consequence, confronted with the fact that they are personally disadvantaged (see Major & Forcey, 1985).

METHODS

In the present chapter we perform secondary analyses of data collected in a survey conducted in Newton, Massachusetts in 1978.[1] Archived at the Henry Murray Center for Research at Radcliffe College, the data set has been described extensively elsewhere (Crosby, 1982, chapter 3 and Appendix II). Our description of the sample and of the measures will therefore be brief.

Sample

Each year Newton publishes an accurate listing of all its adult residents, giving, among other items of information, each person's gender, occupation, and age. From listings of approximately 63,000 names, 394 names of women between the ages of 25 and 40 with high-prestige jobs were found. To be considered "high prestige," occupations needed to have scores of 61.0 or higher on the NORC prestige rating system (Hodge, Siegel, & Rossi, 1964). Names were sorted into two categories on the basis of other information in Newton's "street lists": one category included 177 apparently single women; the other, 277 women who appeared to be married. Names were pulled at random from each category and contacted (by letter and phone) until 31 single women, 30 women with a husband and no children, and 29 women with a husband and at least one child had been reached.

The women in the high-prestige group of the present study had more exalted jobs than is usually true in surveys of professional women (see Etzioni, 1969). Their average NORC prestige rating was over 80. Among the 90 women in the group were 18 physicians; 1 dentist; 12 scientists (e.g., chemist, biostatistician); 2 engineers; 3 architects; 3 administrators; 4 executives; 14 lawyers; 4 consultants; 2 bankers; 11 psychologists; and 14 professors. Assuming that more and more women would have professional careers over the years, the sampling technique intentionally resulted in a sample that was in some sense ahead of its time.

Measures

The measures used in the Newton survey were developed from the theory of relative deprivation and with the original purpose of testing the theory. Table 3.1 presents a summary of the measures developed for each attitude domain (one's own job, the job situation of women generally, one's own home situation). The number of items included in each measure varied. A detailed account of the measures is contained in Crosby (1982, Appendix II). In our analyses all measures were converted to z-scores. We present the standardized scores for expository ease. In fact, the same results would obtain in analyses of raw scores.

Table 3.1

Summary of Measures of Grievance and Related Variables

		Number of Items Used to Assess the Variable on the Topic of:		
Variable Name	High Score Indicates:	Own Job	Women's Job	Own Home Life
Felt deprivation	A great sense of grievance or resentment	4	6	5
Wanting	A gap between actual and desired outcomes	3	3	2
Deserving	A gap between actual outcomes and deserved outcomes	3	2	3
Comparison other	A gap between one's own outcomes and the apparent outcomes of others (or between women's and men's outcomes)	4	3	2
Past expectations	Disappointed expectations	2	2	1
Future expectations	Pessimism about the future	3	3	1
Self-blame	Freedom from self-blame for negative outcomes (or from tendency to blame women)	2	3	1

Critically important for the secondary analyses performed here is a question that was asked after about a quarter-hour of each interview: "In trying to decide how good your own job is, do you ever compare yourself with anyone else?" Of the respondents, 86% said yes and were then asked, "Could you name three people you compare yourself to?" The interviewer wrote down the name or names given and also the gender of the referent person or people. For the respondents who answered the original question in the negative, the interview continued: "Could you right now think of three people who work at the same place as you?" Again, names were taken and genders noted.

Women who named three men in response to these questions were considered to have a male reference group. Women who named only two names, both male, were also considered to have a male reference group. So were women who named one male person and no one else in response to the question. Women who named a male in the first and second positions and a female in the third were also considered to have a predominantly male reference group. Women who named only other women or who named women in the first two positions and a man in the third were considered to have a female reference group. All other combinations (e.g., male first, female second, female third) were considered to be a mixed reference group.

RESULTS

Question 1: Do Any Women
Use a Male Reference Group?

Did any of the career women in the Newton sample use a reference group that was exclusively or predominantly male? The simple answer is yes; 16 of the 90 women in the sample compared themselves exclusively to males. Eight women named three males, 6 named two males and no third choice, and 2 named one male and no other choices. An additional 9 women selected males as their first and second referent person and a female as the third. Thus approximately one out of four women in the sample can be considered to have used a male reference group in deciding how good her own job was. In contrast, 38, or a little more than one woman in three, used a reference group that was exclusively or predominantly female. The remaining 27 women used a mixed reference group.

Question 2: Who Are the Women
with Male Reference Groups?

How did the women with a male reference group differ from those with a female reference group in terms of demographic characteristics? We assessed two job characteristics and two domestic characteristics. On job characteristics we found no difference between the women with a male reference group and those with a female reference group in terms of the prestige ratings of their jobs. We did, however, find a difference in their salaries. The women in our sample with male referents earned significantly more money than did the women with female referents ($F(1, 61) = 7.46$, $p < .01$). Women using mixed groups were intermediate.

Concerning domestic characteristics, we found no difference in household income, but there was a reliable association between reference group and marital status ($\chi^2(4) = 13.70$, $p < .01$). The association between choice of reference group and marital status is depicted in Table 3.2. Here it can be seen that although women with a female reference group tend to be mothers, women with a male reference group are likely to be married but childless. Single women, in contrast, tend to use a mixed reference group. Described in other terms, mothers are more likely to have female (than male) reference groups whereas married but childless women are more likely to have male (than female) reference groups. Single women, in these terms, are more likely to have mixed (than either male or female) reference groups.

Thus the important distinction that differentiated those women who used proportionately female or male reference groups, at least for our sample of professional women, was not whether they are married or single but whether, if married, they did or did not have children.

Question 3: Do Women with a
Male Reference Group Have Distinctive Attitudes?

To answer the third question, we compared the attitudes of the 25 women using a male reference group with the attitudes of the 38

Table 3.2
Frequency of Professional Women Who Employ
Various Reference Groups as a Function of
Marital Status

	Marital Status		
Reference Group	Married Mothers (n = 29)	Married, Childless (n = 30)	Single Women (n = 31)
Male reference group (n = 25)	4	15	6
mixed (n = 27)	8	6	13
Female reference group (n = 38)	17	9	12

women in the sample who use a female reference group. Because the former group differed from the latter in terms of salary, and because one's salary may relate to one's job attitudes, we used salary level as a covariate in the series of one-way analyses of covariance we performed.[2]

Women who used a male reference group differed from women who used a female reference group in terms of their attitudes toward their own jobs. Generally the women who used a male reference group felt more deprived (see columns 1 and 3 of Table 3.3). More specifically, their discontent was revealed in their perceptions of a larger gap between what they have on the one hand and what, on the other hand, they wish to have ($p < .02$), feel entitled to have ($p < .01$), and had expected to have ($p < .01$). Women with a male reference group also tended to be more pessimistic about the future ($p < .08$) and to perceive a large gap between their own outcomes and the outcomes of others ($p < .06$).

The two groups also differed in their job dissatisfaction. In addition to the questions asked about relative deprivation and cognate attitudes, we directly posed two questions about job satisfaction and, because the responses to these questions were highly correlated ($r(88) = .84$, $p < .001$), we created a scale. The women who compared their outcomes exclusively or predominantly to men were significantly more dissatisfied than the women who compared their outcomes to other women ($p < .02$, see last row of Table 3.3).

Although the women with male reference groups differed in their job attitudes from the women with female reference groups, they did not differ at all in their attitudes toward the position of women generally. The lack of parallel between one's own job and that of all women's jobs echoes the lack of parallel found earlier (Crosby, 1982, 1984) between personal deprivation and group deprivation. Nor did the groups differ in their feelings about their home lives: Both groups had relatively positive attitudes about their domestic situation. This last finding (of lack of a finding) indicates that the women who use a male reference group are not simply grumblers who would feel more dissatisfied than other women in every context.

So far it is clear that professional women with male reference groups were more dissatisfied with their jobs than professional women with female reference groups. Thus the one clear prediction from relative deprivation theory was strongly supported. But what about women with a mixed gender reference group? Are these women relatively contented (like women with female reference groups), relatively discontented (like women with male reference groups), or do they hold intermediate attitudes? Unfortunately, relative deprivation theory does not allow us to make a prediction. Nevertheless, because this is an interesting empirical question, we conducted a series of one-way analyses of covariance with all three groups of women. Interestingly, as can be seen in Table 3.3, the women with a mixed reference group (see second column) tended to resemble the women with a male reference group (see first column); they did not resemble the women who compare themselves predominantly to other women (see third column).

DISCUSSION

In this sample of career women many compared themselves exclusively or predominantly to males. Many of these women worked in traditionally male-dominated professions such as medicine, law, and architecture and were probably surrounded by male colleagues. Their use of male reference groups is not, therefore, surprising. But the use of male reference groups cannot be accounted for solely on the basis of the number of males in the profession. A substantial portion of the professional women in the sample used reference groups that were exclusively or predominantly female.

Table 3.3
Mean Scores of Women Using Differing Reference Groups:
Attitudes Toward Own Job in Standardized Scores

	Reference Group		
Variable	Male	Mixed	Female
Felt deprivation	0.14	0.12	−0.14
	(n = 18)	(n = 20)	(n = 27)
Wanting	0.19	−0.02	−0.30
	(n = 24)	(n = 27)	(n = 38)
Deserving	0.34	0.35	−0.13
	(n = 25)	(n = 27)	(n = 38)
Comparison other	0.11	0.24	−0.15
	(n = 25)	(n = 27)	(n = 38)
Past expectations	0.36	0.47	−0.30
	(n = 23)	(n = 27)	(n = 38)
Future expectations	0.13	0.15	−0.20
	(n = 25)	(n = 27)	(n = 37)
Blame	−0.19	−0.32	−0.22
	(n = 18)	(n = 20)	(n = 28)
Job dissatisfaction	0.34	0.19	−0.42
	(n = 25)	(n = 27)	(n = 38)

How much have things changed in the years since the interviews were conducted? Certainly the notion that women should have careers has been steadily gaining acceptance throughout North America. So has the recognition of sex discrimination as a social problem (Kahn & Crosby, 1985). It may therefore be psychologically easier for today's career woman to compare her outcomes to a man's outcomes than it was for yesterday's career woman. On the other hand, the percentage of professional women to use male referents may not be much greater today than it was at the time of the interviews because the realities of sex discrimination, including a sex-segregated work life, have remained much more static than attitudes (Kahn & Crosby, 1985). Even if there has been an increase in the *number* of women who have careers, in short, the nature of work life for those women may not have changed very much since 1978 or 1979.

The great majority of women to use a male reference group were married, childless women. Perhaps a close relationship with a professional man (i.e., their husbands) alerts these women to the possibility of comparing their own outcomes with the outcomes of men similar to themselves. With the arrival of children, however, domestic roles may revert to more gender-stereotyped patterns. Children create domestic labor, and with children the labor may, as never before, become divided. Given the demands of parenthood on professional women, men may cease being "otherwise similar" referents on the job at the same time that the fact of parenthood may establish bonds between professional women and other mothers working in the same environment. Of course, with our cross-sectional data the causal sequence remains unknown. Perhaps women who remain childless differ in a variety of ways from those who seek (or, in any case, accept) motherhood. Perhaps the former are more ambitious than the latter, and their choice of a male reference group is simply one expression of their ambitions.

No easier to unravel, with respect to cause and effect, are the associations between one's reference group and one's job attitudes. Although our main results are consistent with predictions derived from relative deprivation theory, they are correlational in nature. In effect, we have taken a "snapshot" in the ongoing history of career development. Would the "movie version" show what we have implied, that a woman's choice of reference group influences her job attitudes so that a male reference group helps to create discontent? Or do job attitudes somehow influence the choice of reference group? Perhaps it is the disgruntled women who are most likely to look to better-off males as a way of justifying their complaints in their careers. Probably the causal arrow goes in one direction for some women sometimes and in the other direction for others at other times. Future researchers would likely find it rewarding to study the unfolding sequence of events as they occur naturally among selected groups such as professional women.

Indeed, intriguing as the present findings are, they raise more questions than they answer. Why is it, for instance, that women who had male reference groups earned more than those with female reference groups? Given that people fear uncomfortable comparisons, could it be that earning a large salary may in some sense free women to make comparisons with well-paid men?[3] Alternatively, is it not possible that comparisons to men raise a woman's expectations and, hence, demands for a higher salary for herself? Finally, might some third variable, such as achievement motivation or psychological androgyny, relate to both comparisons with male colleagues and higher salaries?

As another example, what is the nature of the connection between work and family life that accounts for the associations we have found between reference groups and marital status? To understand fully the complexities of such connections, researchers will need to perform in-depth qualitative studies of the role of work and family in the lives of North American women. It is hoped that the present study and other, similar quantitative studies can help to lay the foundation for future qualitative research. In such research it will be important to expand the focus of inquiry. For instance, what is the situation of single mothers, a group that was not included in the present study? Will single parenthood force women to compare themselves with other heads of households (i.e., men) and, as a result, feel disadvantaged (see Gutek, Nakamura, Nieva, 1981)? More generally, is the perceived disadvantage that results from comparing with "otherwise similar" men interpreted as sex discrimination, and, if so, does this interpretation lead to other stressful consequences such as increased turnover, which can greatly affect career development (see Greenglass, 1984; Dion, 1986)? Finally, how can discontent be put to good use? How, in other words, can the resentments that are likely to follow cross-gender comparisons be used to promote social justice and help women develop healthy careers? Because the answers to these questions, and others, have great practical significance, continued research is urgently needed.

NOTES

1. The survey was funded by a grant to the second author by the National Institute of Mental Health, RO1-MH31595.

2. A parallel set of one-way analyses of variance revealed an identical pattern of results.

3. Because women with male reference groups were, in fact, *less* disadvantaged (at least compared to the other groups of women), it can be argued that our naturalistic study turned out to be a conservative test of relative deprivation theory. This possibility may, in turn, account for the fact that women with male reference groups were not appreciably more discontented than women with mixed-gender reference groups.

REFERENCES

Crosby, F. (1982). *Relative deprivation and working women.* New York: Oxford University Press.

Crosby, F. (1984). Relative deprivation in organizational settings. *Research in Organizational Behavior* (Vol. 6, pp. 51-93). Greenwich, CT: JAI Press.

Dion, K. L. (1986). Responses to perceived discrimination and relative deprivation. In J. M. Olson, C. P. Herman, & M. P. Zanna (Eds.), *Relative deprivation and social comparison: The Ontario Symposium* (Vol. 4, pp. 159-179). Hillsdale, NJ: Lawrence Erlbaum.

Etzioni, A. (Ed.). (1969). *The semi-professions and their organizations: Teachers nurses, and social workers.* New York: Free Press.

Greenglass, E. R. (1984, August). *Psychological consequences of sex discrimination in female managers.* Paper presented at the annual meeting of the American Psychological Association, Toronto, Ontario.

Gurr, T. R. (1970). *Why men rebel.* Princeton, NJ: Princeton University Press.

Gutek, B. A., Nakamura, C. Y., & Nieva, V. F. (1981). The interdependence of work and family roles. *Journal of Occupational Behavior, 2*, 1-16.

Hodge, R. W., Siegel, P. M., & Rossi, P. H. (1964). Occupational prestige in the United States, 1925-1963. *American Journal of Sociology, 70*, 286-302.

Howe, L. K. (1977). *Pink collar workers.* New York: Putnam.

Kahn, W., & Crosby, F. (1985). Change and stasis: Discriminating between attitudes and discriminating behavior. In L. Larwood, B. A. Gutek, & A. H. Stromberg (Eds.), *Women and work: An annual review* (Vol. 1, pp. 215-238). Beverly Hills, CA: Sage.

Major, B., & Forcey, B. (1985). Social comparisons and pay evaluations: Preferences for same-sex and same-job wage comparisons. *Journal of Experimental Social Psychology, 21*, 393-405.

Merton, R., & Rossi, A. S. (1957). Contributions to the theory of reference group behavior. In R. Merton (Ed.), *Social theory and social structure.* New York: Free Press.

Runciman, W. G. (1966). *Relative deprivation and social justice.* Berkeley: University of California Press.

Stouffer, S. A., Suchman, E. A., DeVinney, L. C., Star, S. A., & Williams, R. M., Jr. (1949). *The American soldier: Adjustment during army life* (Vol. 1). Princeton, NJ: Princeton University Press.

Suls, J. M., & Miller, R. L. (Eds.). (1977). *Social comparison processes.* New York: John Wiley.

4

Now That I Can Have It, I'm Not So Sure I Want It

The Effects of Opportunity on Aspirations and Discontent

JOANNE MARTIN, RAYMOND L. PRICE,
ROBERT J. BIES, and MELANIE E. POWERS

Although women and minorities now have opportunities to enter occupations previously dominated by white males, these opportunities for advancement are often voluntarily refused. Drawing on relative deprivation theory, several reasons for this refusal are examined in an experimental setting. The results shed light on this obstacle to the career development of women and minorities and resolve some contradictions that have plagued the development of relative deprivation theory.

Affirmative action programs attempt to create equal opportunity for women and minorities to increase the representation of these groups in higher-status, higher-paid jobs. It is clear that we have fallen far short of this goal. For example, pay for women is still a fraction of that received by men, irrespective of the way such pay discrepancies are measured (e.g., U.S. Department of Labor, 1983).

Authors' Note: This research was supported in part by a Lena Lake Forrest research fellowship awarded to the senior author by the Business and Professional Women's Foundation.

Research suggests two primary reasons for these discrepancies between men and women. First, females are still often paid less than males holding the same job (e.g., Larwood & Gutek, 1984; Madden, 1985; Mellor, 1984; Pfeffer & Davis-Blake, 1986). Occupational sex segregation is a second, and more substantial, contributing factor. Occupations dominated by women generally pay considerably less than those dominated by men. Furthermore, occupational sex segregation is the rule rather than the exception. For example, Bielby and Baron (1984) studied a diverse sample of 290 California organizations employing about 40,000 males and 11,000 females between 1964 and 1979. Over 90% of these women (or men) would have to change jobs in order to equalize the distribution of their job titles by gender.

Questioning the Desire for Upward Mobility

The paucity of women and minorities in white male-dominated occupations (and, more specifically, jobs) used to be attributed to lack of opportunity. Under the scrutiny of affirmative action programs, however, women and minorities have been given the opportunity to enter many white male-dominated jobs, occupations, and fields of study. Although the successes of affirmative action programs are well documented, a disappointing proportion of these opportunities for advancement have been turned down (Gutek, Larwood, & Stromberg, 1985; Heilman, 1979; U.S. Department of Labor, 1982).

Several explanations for this pattern of voluntary refusal have been offered: the difficulties, such as hostility and discrimination, suffered by those in a solo status (Crocker & McGraw, 1982; Kanter, 1977); lack of appropriate role models (Kram, 1983); the presumption of incompetence that often comes to those whose hiring is attributed to affirmative action preferences rather than to merit (Heilman & Herlihy, 1984; Northcraft & Martin, 1982); and, for women, competing demands for time and energy from husbands, children, and housework (Bernard, 1981; Pleck, 1977). Each of these explanations assumes that if the negative effects of these obstacles could be reduced, women and minorities would want upward mobility. Like some white males, they may not.

Discontent and Aspirations

The desire for upward mobility has two components: discontent with one's current position and a desire for advancement. Without the first, aspirations for advancement may remain vague desires, never enacted. Relative deprivation theory posits that aspirations and discontent are correlated, making this theory potentially useful for addressing the issues described earlier. Unfortunately, results of this research have produced contradictory results concerning the direction of that correlation.

Deprivation is a feeling of discontent, usually operationalized as dissatisfaction or perceived injustice. Some research indicates that improving economic conditions raises hopes for future improvement while increasing discontent with present conditions. Other research suggests the opposite—that chronic lack of improvement and accompanying feelings of futility cause feelings of deprivation. Research supporting both the hope and futility viewpoints is described later.

The hope hypothesis. Relative deprivation research usually focuses on the perspectives of members of disadvantaged groups. The hope hypothesis posits that when economic conditions improve, the disadvantaged should have higher aspirations for upward mobility and should feel more strongly discontent with the status quo. This is the familiar idea that revolutions are caused by rising expectations: "Evils which are patiently endured when they seem inevitable become intolerable once the idea of escape from them is suggested" (de Toqueville, quoted in Davies, 1980, p. 176). Research on collective behavior, such as riots and revolutions, has found some support for the hope hypothesis. For example, as blacks became more prosperous during the 1950s and 1960s, they also became politically more militant and more willing to engage in riots and protests (Crosby, 1976; Lieberson & Silverman, 1970).

These collective behavior studies have generally failed to measure the attitudinal variables, such as aspirations and feelings of discontent, that lie at the core of relative deprivation theory. This is understandable, as it is difficult to obtain measures of the attitudes of participants in the storming of the Bastille or a racial riot. Laboratory experiments, however, have produced evidence supporting the attitudinal components of the hope hypothesis. Holding total outcome levels constant, improving outcomes (usually related to performance on a task) caused higher aspirations and stronger discontent with current outcome levels (Bernstein & Crosby, 1980; Crosby, 1976; Martin, 1978). However, this hope hypothesis has been strongly challenged (see Miller, Bolce, & Halligan, 1977; Tilly, 1978).

The futility hypothesis. There is considerable empirical support for the argument that it is lack of improvement (not improvement) and feelings of futility (not hope) that trigger discontent. Gurr (1970) found that decreases in prosperity were associated with civil strife in 100 polities. Although blacks and whites made substantial economic gains in the 1950s and 1960s, the magnitude of racial inequality did not decrease substantially; this enduring racial inequality, it is argued, caused black unrest (Caplan & Paige, 1968; Pettigrew, 1964, 1967).

Experimental research has also found support for the futility hypothesis. Subjects expressed stronger discontent when achievement of their performance goals seemed more reasonable and less likely (Folger, Rosenfield, & Rheaume, 1983). Large, not small, magnitudes of labor-management pay inequality were associated with greater dissatisfaction and stronger perceptions of injustice by blue-collar workers (Martin, 1981). When outcomes were distributed unequally rather than equally, subjects administered more punishment to a hypothetical elite (Ross, Thibaut, & Evenbeck, 1971). Taken as a whole, this body of research supports the futility hypothesis, which posits that when economic conditions do not improve and opportunities for upward mobility are few, discontent with the status quo will be stronger.

Ideology: The Key to the Contradiction

None of the studies cited earlier contained measures of ideology. Yet it is clear that people differ in their opinions about how valued outcomes, such as money and status, should be distributed. Some ideologies justify unequal distributions. For example, advocates of traditional sex roles assert that women should remain at home or confine themselves to relatively low-status, low-paying occupations (e.g., Schlafly, 1977). Members of disadvantaged groups who endorse these kinds of ideologies should be more likely to have low aspirations for upward mobility and should find reductions in the magnitude of inequality—for example, between male and female pay levels—to be dissatisfying and unjust.

At first glance it may seem surprising that members of disadvantaged groups would endorse an ideology that legitimates their disadvantaged status. However, there is considerable evidence that people will deny the existence of an obvious injustice rather than question their belief that the world is just (Lerner, 1980). This "just world" bias is consistent with the finding that secretaries with little hope of upward mobility often deride the benefits of such advancement and disdain those women who seek promotions out of the secretarial ranks (Kanter, 1977).

Of course, there are ideologies that oppose economic and social discrimination against members of certain groups, such as labor, blacks, ethnic and religious minorities, or women (e.g., Friedan, 1977; Millett, 1969). Members of disadvantaged groups who endorse these ideologies, such as feminist women, should be more likely to desire upward mobility and find larger magnitudes of between-group inequality dissatisfying and unjust.

A few relative deprivation studies have included measures of ideology. For example, Scase (1972) found that British blue-collar workers tended to endorse conservative political ideologies and were likely to consider small magnitudes of labor-management pay inequality dissatisfying and unjust. In contrast, Swedish workers tended to endorse leftist political ideologies and were more likely to consider large labor-management pay differentials to be dissatisfying and unjust. Similar results were found in a study of the racial attitudes and economic discontents of working-class whites in the United States (Vanneman & Pettigrew, 1972).

Such results suggest that ideology may be the missing link that can help explain the contradictory results of previous relative deprivation research. Studies supporting the hope hypothesis—such as de Tocqueville's examination of the American Revolution, or laboratory manipulations of performance outcomes—may have unwittingly focused on contexts in which the dominant, meritocratic ideology legitimized differences between the advantaged and the disadvantaged. Data supporting the futility hypothesis may have been gathered in contexts in which large magnitudes of inequality—for example, between labor and management or blacks and whites—were not considered legitimate according to the dominant ideologies of members of these disadvantaged groups.

If this explanation is correct, ideology should determine whether support for the hope or the futility hypothesis is found. Two experiments testing this contention will be described. The magnitude of inequality—in this case the extent of occupational sex segregation—was manipulated to be large or small. In addition, sex-role ideology (traditional or feminist) was measured. It was predicted, in accord with the futility hypothesis, that feminist women woud find the large magnitude of occupational sex segregation more dissatisfying and unjust and would have stronger desires for upward mobility into a male-dominated occupation. In contrast, it was predicted that the women whose sex-role ideology was more traditional would find smaller magnitudes of inequality more dissatisfying and unjust and would have less desire for upward mobility.

If supported, these predictions would resolve a fundamental contradiction that has troubled the development of relative deprivation theory. In addition, the results would suggest that traditional sex-role attitudes may help explain why some women refuse opportunities for promotions into higher-paid, male-dominated occupations. As will be seen in the results to be reported, however, these predictions underestimate the prevalence of women's resistance to occupational desegregation.

METHOD

Subjects

The subjects in Study I were secretaries at a large insurance company located in California. Subjects in Study II were employed by a second large insurance company located elsewhere in the state. Given that both experiments used similar methodologies, the methodology used in Study I is described below with changes in Study II procedures indicated in parentheses. With one exception, the subjects were female, so the female pronoun is used throughout.

Subjects were randomly selected from the total secretarial pool and were asked to volunteer to participate in a study of secretarial jobs and pay. It was emphasized that the study was being conducted by an independent research team from Stanford University, with no affiliation to or financial support from any company in the insurance industry. All secretaries who were asked to participate did so. The anonymity of their responses was guaranteed. Participation in the study took approximately one hour during an eight-hour shift. At the companies' request, subjects were paid their usual wages and did not receive extra compensation for participation in the study.

Design

In both Studies I and II the level of occupational sex segregation at a company, described in an audiovisual presentation, was manipulated to be large (total segregation) or relatively small (partial integration). In addition, sex-role ideology (traditional or feminist) was used as a blocking variable, yielding a four-group design.

Procedure

Ideology Measure

After a brief introduction, the subjects were asked to complete a questionnaire that included Spence, Helmreich, and Stapp's (1973) measure of sex-role ideology, Attitudes Toward Women in Business. This scale measures levels of agreement with statements concerning, for example, the appropriateness of women's equality with men in business and the professions. Filler items on the questionnaire included measures of locus of control (Patchen, 1961; Rotter, 1966). (These latter items were omitted in Study II due to time constraints.)

Manipulation of Segregation Levels

Next, subjects were shown an audiovisual presentation about a company named Cal Oil. The audio portion of the presentation described the daily routines of employees who held one of two jobs: secretary or sales manager. The video portion of the presentation consisted of slides containing the experimental manipulations of occupational sex segregation. Slides of three executives were shown. In the totally segregated condition all three of these executives were male. In the partially integrated condition one of the executives was a female, and the other two executives were male.[1] Slides of three female secretaries were also shown, the same in both conditions. Subjects were randomly assigned to condition. Gender was not mentioned in the audiovisual presentation or in the dependent measures in order to minimize social desirability biases in subjects' responses.

Although Cal Oil was a fictitious name, the company was real and the job descriptions were taken almost verbatim from transcripts of interviews with people who actually held these positions. The secretarial job at Cal Oil closely resembled the jobs held by the experimental subjects, who were instructed to view the presentation from the perspective of a secretary at Cal Oil. (In Study II to enhance the impact of the experimental manipulation, subjects were asked to imagine they would be working for the individual sales managers pictured in the slides.)

In spite of these similarities to the subjects' working situations, the subjects did not work at Cal Oil. This fact strengthened the design of the study in several ways. First, because the study focused on a potentially explosive topic, we had to agree not to question the subjects about their personal feelings concerning their current positions and pay levels. Thus the fact that the experimental materials focused on jobs and pay at Cal Oil made it possible to obtain access to these secretarial subjects. Second, the focus on Cal Oil made it possible to manipulate the level of occupational sex segregation. It is highly unlikely that such a manipulation would otherwise be feasible or ethical in a field setting. Third, this aspect of the design alleviated subjects' concerns about the anonymity of their responses. Finally, this design reduced some sources of error variance, such as subjects' idiosyncratic feelings about their bosses or their personal pay histories.

After the audiovisual presentation was shown, subjects in both conditions were given a pay plan consisting of the highest, average, and lowest pay levels for secretaries ($245, $220, $195 a week, respectively) and for sales managers ($625, $600, $575 a week, respectively). (In Study II pay levels were multiplied by four and labeled as monthly salaries, as this company paid its secretaries on a monthly basis.) These pay levels had been carefully pretested to ensure that they corresponded realistically to pay scales at the subjects' places of work. When these pay levels had been examined, the subjects were asked to respond to a questionnaire that contained the dependent measures and manipulation checks.

Dependent Measures

All these measures required the subject to consider how a secretary at Cal Oil would feel if she earned the average pay level for secretaries there. Two kinds of dependent variables—feelings of relative deprivation and aspirations—were measured.

Five items measured feelings of deprivation concerning the pay levels at Cal Oil. The first, general measure asked subjects to rate the average pay level for secretaries at Cal Oil on a 9-point scale, with endpoints labeled "much more than deserved" and "much less than deserved." The remaining relative deprivation measures forced a comparison either to other secretarial or to sales managers' pay levels. The subjects were asked to rate on 9-point scales the extent to which they found each comparison dissatisfying or unjust.

For example, one of these items was worded as follows: "Compare the earnings of the secretaries as a group to the earnings of the sales managers as a group. If you were a secretary, earning the average pay for secretaries, $220 a week, how would you feel about the way these earnings compare?" For this item the scale endpoints were labeled "completely dissatisfied" and "completely satisfied." The other deprivation measures were comparably worded.[2]

The aspiration measures assessed the likelihood and desirability of upward mobility into the executive position. The subjects were asked to rate the likelihood that they personally would be promoted into a sales manager position at Cal Oil. (In Study II they were also asked to rate the likelihood that any secretary at Cal Oil, not just the subject personally, would be offered a promotion into the executive ranks.) In addition, the subjects were asked how much they would desire a promotion into a sales manager position at Cal Oil. A similarly worded question asked about the desirability of an unspecified, nonsecretarial promotion at Cal Oil. Subjects responded to all these items on 9-point scales, with endpoints labeled "extremely likely" and "extremely unlikely" or "not at all" and "very much," as appropriate.

Manipulation Checks

These items were located at the end of the questionnaire in order to preclude any influence on responses to the dependent measures. For the purpose of conducting a manipulation check, subjects were asked to estimate the demographic characteristics (age and education level, as well as gender) of the secretaries and executives at Cal Oil.

Debriefing

Upon completion of the questionnaire, the subjects were given a partial explanation of the study. After all subjects had participated and the data had been analyzed, a more detailed written explanation, including some of the study's findings, was made available to subjects. Results from Study I and II are now presented.

STUDY I

Results

Subjects

The subjects in Study I were 69 secretaries, all of whom worked full-time at the same large insurance company. Demographic data on the subject sample were collected. The subjects' average age was 37 years. Approximately half the sample had obtained a high school diploma; a third had done some college work or had completed a college degree. In order to protect their anonymity, the secretaries were asked to identify a range, rather than their exact salary levels. The mean was a category ranging from $201 to $250 a week, before taxes and not including overtime. This figure was comparable with the average pay for secretaries, $220 a week, used in the Cal Oil stimulus materials.

Manipulation Checks

The manipulation of the levels of occupational sex segregation was clearly successful. Subjects estimated, on average, that the percentage of male sales managers was 99.7% in the totally segregated condition (three male slides) and 77.9% in the partially integrated condition (one female and two male slides).[3] This difference was significant, $t(64) = 8.66$, $p < .0001$. Although the estimated percentages reflect the sex ratios in the stimulus materials, the percentage of female executives is clearly underestimated in the partial integration condition.

Ideology

Scores on the Attitudes Toward Women in Business scale were split at the median, dividing subjects in each of the two conditions (total segregation and partial integration) into two groups: "traditionals" and "feminists." The ideological orientations of these two groups are not highly divergent, as few extremely feminist or traditional scores were recorded. (The analyses to be reported were repeated using three-group and continuous coding of the ideological data. The results were not significantly different.)

Dependent Variables

The cell means for each of the dependent measures in Study I are presented in Table 4.1. A series of two-by-two unweighted means analyses of variance were performed. The independent variables in these analyses were level of occupational sex segregation (totally segregated or partially integrated) and ideology (traditional or feminist). All analyses were repeated using the subjects' year of birth and personal salary ranges as covariates. The results of these analyses of covariance were not significantly different from those reported later and so are not reported.

Relative deprivation. For each of the five measures of relative deprivation it was predicted that feminist subjects would express more discontent in the totally segregated than in the partially integrated condition. The opposite pattern of results was predicted for the traditional subjects. The analyses of variance for these five dependent measures yielded few significant main effects or interactions. For each measure the direction of the effects is similar. Therefore, after the results of the analyses of variance are summarized, the direction of the observed effects will be discussed for all five measures together.

Table 4.1
Mean Level of Relative Deprivation and Aspiration:
Study I

	Totally Segregated		Partially Segregated	
	Traditional (n = 17)[2]	Feminist (n = 21)	Traditional (n = 12)	Feminist (n = 19)
Relative deprivation:[1]				
Pay less than deserved	3.65[b]	2.00[a]	2.45[ab]	2.16[a]
Dissatisfied in comparison to other secretaries	4.53[b]	2.86[a]	4.75[b]	4.11[ab]
Perceived injustice in comparison to other secretaries	4.00[a]	3.48[a]	4.50[a]	3.58[a]
Dissatisfaction in comparison to executives	3.47[ab]	2.05[a]	3.58[b]	3.37[ab]
Perceived injustice in comparison to executives	4.06[a]	2.86[a]	3.42[a]	3.63[a]
Level of Aspiration:[1]				
Likelihood of self being promoted	4.59[a]	3.71[a]	4.92[a]	4.26[a]
Desirability of promotion into nonsecretrarial position	7.82[a]	7.85[a]	7.08[a]	7.63[a]
Desirability of promotion into a managerial position	6.47[a]	7.19[a]	6.50[a]	6.95[a]

1. Smaller numbers indicate pay is less than deserved, more dissatisfying, and perceived as more unjust, promotions are less likely and less desirable. Row means not sharing a common superscript differ at $p < .05$ or better (Duncan's multiple range test).
2. Number of subjects per cell was unequal because scores in the sex-role ideology scale were split at the median and used as a blocking variable.

The first, general measure of relative deprivation asked subjects to assess the extent to which secretarial pay levels at Cal Oil were less than deserved. This measure produced the strongest differences among the four groups of subjects. The main effect for level of segregation was not significant; the main effect for ideology was significant ($F(1, 65) = 7.83$, $p < .01$); and the interaction between level of segregation and ideology was marginally significant ($F(1, 65) = 3.46$, $p < .10$).

The remaining measures specified the comparative sources of these feelings of relative deprivation. Subjects were asked to assess their dissatisfaction and feelings of injustice in relation to the pay levels of other secretaries at Cal Oil. For this measure of dissatisfaction the main effect for level of segregation was not significant, the main effect for ideology was significant ($F(1, 68) = 4.79$, $p < .05$), and the interaction was not significant. For this measure of injustice the main effects for level of segregation and ideology and the interaction were not significant.

Subjects were also asked to assess their dissatisfaction and feelings of injustice in relation to the pay levels of the sales managers at Cal Oil. For this measure of dissatisfaction, the main effect for level of segregation was not significant, the main effect for ideology was marginally significant ($F(1, 64) = 3.16$, $p < .10$), and the interaction was not significant. For this measure of injustice the main effect for level of segregation, the main effect for ideology, and the interaction were not significant.

Contrary to predictions, moderate amounts of discontent were expressed by all four groups of subjects. Inspection of the means for all five of these dependent measures suggested that feminists exposed to total segregation expressed stronger feelings of relative deprivation than the other three groups of subjects. Contrasts[4] of the feminists in the totally segregated condition to the other three groups indicated that the former were significantly more likely to feel that secretarial pay levels at Cal Oil were less than deserved ($t(65) = 2.10$, $p < .02$), significantly more likely to feel dissatisfied with comparisons to other secretarial pay levels ($t(66) = 2.67$, $p < .005$), marginally more likely to find those secretarial pay levels unjust ($t(66) = 1.01$, $p < .10$), significantly more likely to be dissatisfied with comparisons to executive pay levels ($t(50) = 3.42$, $p < .0005$), and marginally more likely to find those executive pay levels unjust ($t(66) = 1.60$, $p < .06$).

Level of aspiration. A similar pattern of results was observed in the levels of aspiration data. No significant main effects or interactions were found. For subjects in all four groups, estimates of the likelihood and desirability of promotion hovered near the midpoint of the scales. Comparisons of the feminists in the totally segregated condition to the other three groups indicated that the former considered promotions into the sales manager position marginally less likely ($t(66) = 1.42$, $p < .10$) and slightly, but not significantly, more desirable (both $t < 1$).

Discussion

The results of Study I produced limited support for the futility hypothesis; discontent was generally stronger, and aspirations were slightly higher among feminist subjects exposed to total segregation rather than partial integration. However, level of segregation did not have the expected effect on subjects whose sex-role ideology was more traditional. In both the total segregation and the partial integration conditions, traditional subjects had relatively low levels of discontent and aspiration (a pattern of results quite like that of the feminists exposed to partial integration). Perhaps because these traditional subjects did not approve of executive roles for women, their feelings about their pay and chances of upward mobility were unaffected by the proportion of female executives. Thus only one of the four groups of subjects expressed the combination of high aspirations and strong discontent predicted by the futility hypothesis.

This is an interesting pattern of results because only one of the four groups showed an intense emotional reaction to occupational sex segregation. The traditional women certainly did not register the strong disapproval of integration that we had predicted. One of the more traditional subjects in Study I offered an explanation for her apparent lack of involvement. After the debriefing session she said, "You know, what you academics don't understand is that we have to learn to live with dissatisfaction." Such resignation is congruent with the results of research indicating that disadvantaged people sometimes come to see their situation as just or even desirable (e.g., Lerner, 1980; Kanter, 1977). The lack of emotional involvement on the part of traditional subjects may therefore be easier to understand than the reactions of the feminist subjects to partial integration. Why were they expressing the same low levels of aspiration and discontent as the traditional subjects?

Before addressing these questions about the meaning of these results, it is essential to acknowledge limitations of this first study that necessitated the conduct of a second study. The results of Study I were relatively weak. In order to facilitate comparison of the results of Study I and II, the report of the results of Study I included the results of a series of t-tests. Such tests are usually reserved for planned comparisons, and the pattern of results observed in Study I was only partially anticipated by the predictions. When a more conservative statistic (the Duncan multiple range test) was used, few of these differences among the groups were significant, as reported in Table 4.1.

Problems concerning the strengths of the observed effects were compounded by concerns about generalizability. All the subjects in Study I worked for the same organization, and it is possible that some unanticipated characteristic of that firm's employment policies affected the responses of the subject sample. For these reasons a second study was conducted, using subjects from a different company. Minor changes in the procedure were made, as noted in the earlier methods section, to increase the personal relevance and impact of the study materials. It was hoped that these minor changes would strengthen the observed effects.

STUDY II

Results

Subjects

The subjects were 68 female secretaries from a second large insurance company. Due to time constraints, no demographic data were collected from these subjects.

Design

A one-way, four-group design was used in order to permit a planned contrast between feminists in the total segregation condition and the subjects in the other three groups: feminists in the partial integration condition, traditionals in the total segregation condition, and traditionals in the partial integration condition.

Manipulation Checks

As in Study I, the experimental manipulation was successful. In the totally segregated condition subjects estimated, on the average, that 99.7% of the sales managers were male. In the partially integrated condition they estimated that 74.6% were male. This difference between the conditions was significant (t(64) = 9.02, p < .0001). As in the first study, the percentage of female sales managers in the partially integrated condition was underestimated.

Ideology

As in Study I, subjects' responses to the scale measuring sex-role ideology were used as a blocking variable. Scores were again split at the median, dividing subjects within each of the experimental conditions into two groups: feminists and traditionals.

Dependent Variables

The cell means for each of the dependent measures for Study II are presented in Table 4.2.

Relative deprivation. The relative deprivation measures generally followed the pattern observed in Study I. The feminists in the totally segregated condition, in contrast to the other three groups of subjects, were significantly more likely to feel that secretarial pay levels at Cal Oil were less than deserved (t(64) = 2.49, p < .01), significantly more likely to feel dissatisfied with comparisons to other secretarial pay levels (t(63) = 1.93, p < .03) slightly but not significantly more likely to find those secretarial pay levels unjust (t < 1), significantly more likely to be dissatisfied with comparisons to sales managers' pay levels (t(42) = 4.05, p < .0001), and significantly more likely to find those sales managers' pay levels unjust (t(63) = 1.66, p < .05).

Level of aspiration. Feminists in the totally segregated condition rated their personal chances of promotion into the sales manager position as significantly less likely than subjects in the other three groups (t(62) = 2.47, p < .01). This planned comparison was also significant for the likelihood of secretaries in general being promoted (t(64) = 2.02, p < .03). Results concerning the desirability of promotions followed a similar pattern. Feminists in the totally segregated condition, in contrast to subjects in the other three groups, rated promotions into unspecified, nonsecretarial positions and into sales manager positions as significantly more desirable (t(57) = –4.37, p < .0001 and t(57) = –5.87, p < .0001, respectively).

Table 4.2
Mean Level of Relative Deprivation and Aspiration:
Study II

	Totally Segregated		Partially Segregated	
	Traditional (n = 18)[2]	Feminist (n = 14)	Traditional (n = 17)	Feminist (n = 19)
Relative deprivation:[1]				
Pay less than deserved	2.89[b]	1.79[a]	2.76[b]	2.95[b]
Dissatisfied in comparison to other secretaries	3.61[b]	3.00[a]	4.29[b]	4.67[b]
Perceived injustice in comparison to other secretaries	3.94[a]	3.93[a]	4.76[a]	4.79[a]
Dissatisfaction in comparison to executives	2.89[b]	1.50[a]	2.82[b]	3.16[b]
Perceived injustice in comparison to executives	3.11[b]	2.36[a]	3.69[b]	3.16[b]
Level of aspiration:[1]				
Likelihood of self being promoted	2.33[b]	2.36[a]	3.94[b]	4.90[b]
Likelihood of any secretary being promoted	2.44[b]	2.31[a]	4.58[b]	4.44[b]
Desirability of promotion into nonsecretarial position	7.56[b]	8.79[a]	6.53[b]	7.42[b]
Desirability of promotion into executive position	5.83[b]	8.61[a]	5.18[b]	6.26[b]

1. Smaller numbers indicate pay is less than deserved, more dissatisfying, and perceived as more unjust, promotions are less likely and less desirable. Row means not sharing a common superscript differ at p < .05 or better (t-test).
2. Number of subjects per cell was unequal because scores in the sex-role ideology scale were split at the median and used as a blocking variable. Cell sizes vary slightly for some dependent measures due to missing data.

Discussion

In Study II, as in Study I, feminist secretaries in the totally segregated condition, in contrast to the other three groups of subjects, expressed significantly more relative deprivation and rated promotions out of the secretarial ranks as significantly less likely and significantly more desirable. As in Study I, traditional secretaries were unaffected by the level of occupational sex segregation, expressing relatively low levels of discontent and aspirations (results again similar to those of the feminist secretaries exposed to partial integration).

Implications for Relative Deprivation Theory

The reactions of the feminist secretaries to total occupational sex segregation fit the futility hypothesis: Lack of hope for improvement caused intense discontent accompanied by a strong desire for upward mobility. The results of these two studies suggest that relative deprivation researchers examining the hope and futility hypotheses should include consideration of ideology. Futility should heighten discontent and raise aspirations only among those whose ideology endorses the need for change. People whose ideology supports the current state of affairs should be content if no change, or small change, occurs.

Integrating Ideology into Affirmative Action Programs

The results of these studies also have implications for the career development of women and minorities. Those who believe in ideologies that make upward mobility undesirable may be particularly likely to refuse opportunities for advancement through affirmative action programs, even though they could benefit. Thus ideology may be a serious obstacle to the effectiveness of affirmative action programs, particularly among certain target populations, such as those blue-collar women who endorse traditional sex roles (see O'Farrell & Harlan, 1982).

There are practical implications that follow from this conclusion. Rather than focusing exclusively on hiring and promotion policies, some affirmative action programs may find it useful to focus directly on ideology. It may be helpful to determine if targeted individuals or groups of women and minorities endorse ideologies that undermine (or emphasize) the attractiveness of upward mobility. Information about ideology could be used to direct limited affirmative action resources more effectively. It might even be possible to find ethical and effective ways to challenge ideologies that oppose upward mobility for members of disadvantaged groups, perhaps by presenting data that undermine the assumption that the world is just (see Lerner, 1975).

Questioning the Effectiveness of Partial Integration

The results of these two studies also have implications concerning the alleged helpfulness of partial integration as a step toward total integration. Previous research, cited in the introduction to this chapter, has effectively demonstrated that partial integration has detrimental effects on the few members of a disadvantaged group who join a more advantaged group. These negative effects are often justified by claims that these "pioneers" are providing role models for those who remain behind in a disadvantaged position, raising the latter's aspirations for mobility. The results of the present studies suggest that partial integration may also have negative effects on those who remain behind.

In Studies I and II occupational sex integration efforts were surprisingly unsuccessful at encouraging desire for upward mobility or discontent with the status quo. Partial integration had little effect on the discontent and aspiration levels of those traditional secretaries whose ideology supported occupational sex segregation. Moreover, it is possible that partial integration actually lowered the aspiration levels of those feminist secretaries whose ideology was opposed to segregation, making them more content with their current, disadvantaged position.

The ideological recommendations discussed here may be helpful in alleviating negative reactions to partial integration that come from women and minorities whose traditional ideologies oppose integration efforts. However, these recommendations are useless for those feminist women who ideologically endorse upward mobility but do not seem to want it when it becomes available. This problem is explored in the next section.

The Reactance Paradox

The reactions of the feminist secretaries to the partial integration condition present a paradox. It is as if these women were saying, in accord with reactance theory (Wortman & Brehm, 1975), "Now that I can have it, I don't want it as much." At least four explanations for this phenomenon come to mind: practicality, devaluation, vicarious achievement, and the "tunnel effect."

The simplest explanation is the most practical: People may not seriously assess the negative aspects of upward mobility until such mobility becomes a real possibility. Only at that point will the costs become evident. For example, until an executive promotion is likely, a female secretary may not consider such costs as longer hours, the stress of increased responsibility, or the difficulties of coping with sexual harassment and other forms of discrimination.

A second, quite pessimistic explanation is based on the premise that objects, such as jobs, may be devalued when they are in plentiful supply (Worchel, Lee, & Adewole, 1975). Thus when a job becomes accessible to members of a disadvantaged group, they may devalue it and consider its prestige lowered (Touhey, 1974). For example, the presence of female executives may make that executive position seem less prestigious to female secretaries.

A third explanation is that feminists who see other women advance into previously all-male positions may be happy for them and conclude that discrimination against women is no longer a problem. Thus whatever lack of advancement these women experience must be their own fault. A variant of this explanation emphasizes vicarious achievement. Rather than serving as role models, the newly promoted, ex-members of a disadvantaged group may serve as substitute sources of gratification. For example, some female secretaries may react to the presence of a female executive by thinking, "Since she is representing females in the executive ranks, I can be more content with my secretarial position."

A fourth explanation suggests that feminist contentment with partial integration may be a transient phenomenon, if it becomes clear that discrimination against women is in fact still a problem. This last explanation is consistent with Hirschman's (1973) "tunnel effect" hypothesis. The tunnel effect is a metaphor about a car held up by a traffic jam in a tunnel. The first reaction to seeing a parallel lane of traffic move in the desired direction of travel should be satisfaction. The source of this satisfaction is the anticipation that soon the currently halted lane of traffic will also begin moving. As in the present studies, improvement of the status of similar others should alleviate discontent and raise aspirations. However, Hirschman hypothesizes that this contentment will turn into bitter discontent if aspirations continue to be frustrated and the halted lane of traffic does not eventually begin to move. The tunnel effect explanation suggests that partial integration may only temporarily alleviate discontent. If aspirations for improvement are not met, partial integration may eventually bring severe discontent.

Each of these four explanations provides an intriguing direction for future research. If partial integration does have the paradoxical effect of temporarily or more permanently decreasing discontent and lowering aspirations among those whose ideology sanctions upward mobility, it would be useful to explore the limits of this phenomenon and find out why it occurs.

NOTES

1. Partial integration often begins with the inclusion of a single disadvantaged individual into an advantaged group. The detrimental effects of such a solo position, such as biased performance evaluations, have been well documented (e.g., Crocker & McGraw, 1982; Taylor, Fiske, Etcoff, & Ruderman, 1978). If partial integration proceeds further toward full integration, a few more members from the disadvantaged group enter the advantaged group. At a point short of full integration, a critical mass is reached, it becomes clearer to observers that all members of the disadvantaged group are not alike, and the detrimental effects of minority status begin to disappear (Kanter, 1977). Partial integration, as operationalized in this chapter, is most probably a point between the solo and critical mass positions. (See note 4.)

To determine if the physical attractiveness of the single female executive affected the results, two versions of the partially integrated condition were run, varying the woman pictured as the female executive. Analysis of the data in Studies I and II indicated no differences due to this variation, so the data from these two conditions were merged.

2. Additional dependent measures asked subjects about other aspects of work at Cal Oil. For example, subjects were asked to assess the importance of various nonfinancial rewards, such as work with interesting people; the extent of their loyalty to their bosses; and the level of effort they would put into their work. The variance of responses to these other dependent measures was very small. The few significant between-group differences found in Study I were not replicated in Study II, so these variables will not be discussed further.

3. This latter percentage (22.1% female) approaches the usual estimates of critical mass for minorities (Kanter, 1977; Martin & Pettigrew, 1984), although the results of the studies reported in this chapter suggest that the detrimental effects of minority status have not yet disappeared. It would be interesting to vary the level of partial integration systematically, in order to determine the turning point at which detrimental effects begin to disappear.

4. The contrasts in Studies I and II assign a weight of –3 to the feminists in the total segregation condition and a weight of +1 to the other three groups. Because predictions specify the direction of the effect, one-tailed tests were used. When the Bartlett-Box test indicated that the variances were not homogeneous, the test was based on separate variance estimates. Thus there is some variation in the appropriate degrees of freedom.

REFERENCES

Bernard, J. (1981). *The female world*. New York: Free Press.
Bernstein, M., & Crosby, F. (1980). An empirical investigation of relative deprivation theory. *Journal of Experimental Social Psychology, 16*, 442-456.
Bielby, W. T., & Baron, J. N. (1984). A woman's place is with other women: Sex segregation within organizations. In B. F. Reskin (Ed.), *Sex segregation in the workplace: Trends, explanations, remedies*. Washington, DC: National Academy Press.
Caplan, N., & Paige, J. M. (1968). A study of ghetto rioters. *Scientific American, 219*, 15-22.
Crocker, J., & McGraw, K. M. (1982). What's good for the goose is not good for the gander: Solo status as an obstacle to occupational achievement for males and females. *American Behavioral Scientist, 27*, 357-369.
Crosby, F. (1976). A model of egoistical relative deprivation. *Psychological Review, 83*, 85-113.
Davies, J. C. (1980). Toward a theory of revolution. In M. D. Pugh (Ed.), *Collective behavior: A source book*. St. Paul, MN: West.
Folger, R., Rosenfield, D., & Rheaume, K. (1983). Roleplaying effects of likelihood and referent outcomes on relative deprivation. *Representative Research in Social Psychology, 13*, 2-10.
Friedan, B. (1977). *The feminine mystique*. New York: Norton.
Gurr, T. R. (1970). *Why men rebel*. Princeton, NJ: Princeton University Press.
Gutek, B., Larwood, L., & Stromberg, A. (1985). Women at work. In C. Cooper & I. Robertson (Eds.), *Review of industrial/organizational psychology* (Vol. 1). Chichester, England: John Wiley.
Heilman, M. E. (1979). High school students' occupational interest as a function of projected sex ratios in male-dominated occupations. *Journal of Applied Psychology, 64*, 275-279.
Heilman, M. E., & Herlihy, J. M. (1984). Affirmative action, negative reaction? Some moderating conditions. *Organizational Behavior and Human Performance, 33*, 204-213.
Hirschman, A. O. (1973). The changing tolerance for income inequality in the course of economic development. *Quarterly Journal of Economics, 87*, 544-566.
Kanter, R. M. (1977). *Men and women of the corporation*. New York: Basic Books.
Kram, K. E. (1983). Phases of the mentor relationship. *Academy of Management Journal, 26*, 608-625.

Larwood, L., & Gutek, B. A. (1984). Women at work in the USA. In M. J. Davidson & C. C. Cooper (Eds.), *Working women: An international survey*. Chichester, England: John Wiley.

Lerner, M. J. (1975). The justice motive in social behavior. *Journal of Social Issues, 31*, 1-20.

Lerner, M. J. (1980). *The belief in a just world: A fundamental delusion*. New York: Plenum.

Lieberson, S., & Silverman, A. R. (1970). The precipitants and underlying conditions of race riots. In F. I. Megaree & J. E. Hokanson (Eds.), *The dynamics of aggression*. New York: Harper & Row.

Madden, J. (1985). The persistence of pay differentials: The economics of sex discrimination. In L. Larwood, A. H. Stromberg, & B. A. Gutek (Eds.), *Women and work: An annual review* (Vol. 1). Beverly Hills, CA: Sage.

Martin, J. (1978, August). *The effects of rate of change in performance*. Paper presented at the annual meeting of the American Psychological Association, Toronto, Canada.

Martin J. (1981). Relative deprivation: A theory of distributive injustice for an era of shrinking resources. In L. Cummings & B. Staw (Eds.), *Research in organizational behavior* (Vol. 3). Greenwich, CT: JAI Press.

Martin, J., & Pettigrew, T. F. Shaping the organizational context for minority inclusion. *Journal of Social Issues* (accepted pending revision).

Mellor, E. F. (1984). Investigating the differences in weekly earnings of men and women. *Monthly Labor Review, 107*, 17-28.

Miller, A. H., Bolce, L. H., & Halligan, M. (1977). The J-curve theory and the Black urban riots. *American Political Science Review, 71*, 964-982.

Millett, K. (1969). *Sexual politics*. New York: Doubleday.

Northcraft, G., & Martin, J. (1982). Double jeopardy: Resistance to affirmative action from potential beneficiaries. In B. A. Gutek (Ed.), *Sex-role stereotyping and affirmative action policy*. Los Angeles: UCLA Institute for Industrial Relations.

O'Farrell, B., & Harlan, S. L. (1982). Craftworkers and clerks: The effect of male co-worker hostility on women's satisfaction with non-traditional jobs. *Social Problems, 23*, 252-294.

Patchen, M. (1961). *The choice of wage comparisons*. Englewood Cliffs, NJ: Prentice-Hall.

Pettigrew, T. F. (1964). *A profile of the Negro American*. New York: Van Nostrand.

Pettigrew, T. F. (1967). Social evaluation theory: Convergence and applications. In D. Levine (Ed.), *Nebraska Symposium on Motivation* (Vol. 15). Lincoln: University of Nebraska Press.

Pfeffer, J., & Davis-Blake, A. (1986). The effect of the proportion of women on salaries: The case of college administrators. *Administrative Science Quarterly, 31*.

Pleck, J. H. (1977). The work-family role system. *Social Problems, 24*, 417-427.

Ross, M., Thibaut, J., & Evenbeck, S. (1971). Some determinants of the intensity of social protest. *Journal of Experimental Social Psychology, 7*, 401-418.

Rotter, J. B. (1966). Generalized expectancies for internal versus external control of reinforcement. *Psychological Monographs, 80*(1), (Whole No. 607).

Scase, R. (1972). Relative deprivation: A comparison of English and Swedish manual workers. In D. Wedderburn (Ed.), *Poverty, inequality, and class structure*. Cambridge: Cambridge University Press.

Schlafly, P. (1977). *The power of the positive woman*. New Rochelle, NY: Arlington House.

Spence, J. T., Helmreich, R., & Stapp, J. (1973). A short version of the Attitudes Toward Women Scale (AWS). *Bulletin of the Psychonomic Society, 2*, 219-220.

Taylor, S. E., Fiske, S. T., Etcoff, N. L., & Ruderman, A. J. (1978). Categorical and contextual bases of person memory and stereotyping. *Journal of Personality and Social Psychology, 36*, 778-793.

Tilly, C. (1978). *From mobilization to revolution*. Reading, MA: Addison-Wesley.

Touhey, J. C. (1974). Effects of additional women professionals on ratings of occupational prestige and desirability. *Journal of Personality and Social Psychology, 29*(1), 86-89.

U.S. Department of Labor. (1982). *Employment and earnings*. Washington, DC: U.S. Bureau of Labor Statistics.

U.S. Department of Labor. (1983). *Time of change: 1983 handbook on women workers*. Bulletin 298. Washington, DC: U.S. Department of Labor.

Vanneman, R. D., & Pettigrew, T. F. (1972). Race and relative deprivation in the urban United States. *Race, 13*, 461-486.

Worchel, S., Lee, J., & Adewole, A. (1975). Effects of supply and demand on ratings of object value. *Journal of Personality and Social Psychology, 32*, 906-914.

Wortman, C. B., & Brehm, J. W. (1975). Responses to uncontrollable outcomes: An integration of the reactance theory and the learned helplessness model. In L. Berkowitz (Ed.), *Advances in experimental social psychology* (Vol. 8). New York: Academic Press.

5

Successful Women
A Psychological Investigation of
Family Class and Education Origins

SUSAN K. BOARDMAN, CHARLES C. HARRINGTON,
and SANDRA V. HOROWITZ

As part of an exploratory study investigating life-history antecedents of career success for 100 men and women, 49 women were extensively interviewed. The sample consists of 25 black and 24 white females between the ages of 40 and 55 who had achieved extraordinary levels of occupational success in business, academia, or government service. Of these, 29, whom we label "negative prediction defiers" (NPDs), grew up in low socioeconomic families with parents who did not complete high school. Twenty "controls" came from middle-class or higher backgrounds. Analyses of interview data on selected variables reveal general tendencies for both groups to employ constructive defenses in dealing with stress and to exhibit strong achievement motivation, strong reward orientation, and an internal locus of control. NPDs were found to differ from controls in having lower reward orientation, more internal locus of control, and a greater linkage between personal and professional friendship patterns. Results are discussed in relation to situational difficulties posed by socioeconomic status and race. Costs incurred in attaining success are also discussed.

The United States is a stratified society that presents a variety of barriers to an equal distribution of its opportunities as well as its resources. Skin color and socioeconomic class of origin, gender, and

Authors' Note: An earlier version of this chapter was presented at the 92nd Annual Meeting of the American Psychological Association. Research was funded by a grant from the Spencer Foundation, "Negative Prediction Defiers: Education Antecedents of Success," directed by Charles C. Harrington.

language are examples of characteristics that are good statistical predictors of success. Despite the negative predictions based upon such factors, many people born black, Hispanic, female, or poor do achieve high levels of occupational status and career success. Simply stated, the purpose of this study is to find out how they do it. Although being black and/or female are themselves negative predictors of career success, in this study we examine women who defy the additional negative predictions attached to their having come from economically and educationally disadvantaged households. We compare them with equally successful women who grew up in more traditionally middle-class households.

Many studies have examined the entry points and career options for blacks and women, but the study of these phenomena retrospectively for highly successful careers has been largely neglected (for exceptions see Nieva & Gutek, 1981). The question is, How is success achieved in the face of society's negative expectations?

Our impetus for conducting such research has been twofold. First, we want to redress an imbalance in a literature that has examined failure for these groups more than it has the reverse. Second, we focus on midlife career status, taking a long-term view not measured by input-output studies of performance over brief periods of time. We are convinced by recent work of Vaillant (1977) and Levinson et al. (1978) that examination of careers that are well under way is essential.

We therefore conducted a retrospective study enabling us to assess the relevance of schooling and economic status of the family of origin to successful work careers in people now aged 40-55 whose careers are firmly established. We need to examine what and how opportunities develop, but we are also sensitive to the possibility that opportunities contribute only to those able to make use of them. In this chapter we will report results for the psychological variables we have examined in these contexts. As these phenomena are so little studied it is appropriate that our research be largely exploratory. It is hoped that our analyses will allow the planning of later confirmatory (e.g., survey) designs.

The larger research examines the work, educational, and family histories of highly successful black and white men and women "negative prediction defiers" (NPDs) in order to identify how these outstanding careers were constructed, what made a difference, and how individuals were able to respond to opportunities. Comparisons are made between subjects coming from two kinds of households: economically and educationally disadvantaged (the NPDs) and households more traditionally middle class (the controls). For the two groups we examine and compare the personal resources these people have brought to their life tasks—their motivational orientations, styles of coping with stress and frustration, and so on. We also compare the networks of family and peer support and the kinds of serendipity that may have served as turning points in these persons' lives. Finally, we discuss how these factors interact to influence the decisions and actions of the two groups and the *processes* that have been involved in their success.

Career Development and Personality

In examining variations in responses to opportunity, one of the primary psychological variables linked to career success is achievement motivation. This work, begun by McClelland, Atkinson, and their colleagues in the early 1950s, was intended to explain stable tendencies in certain persons oriented toward striving for "success in life." The research of these investigators suggests that people who are relatively high in achievement motivation tend to attempt tasks that appear moderately difficult to them (rather than easy or extremely difficult); tend to be persistent in the face of difficulties they may encounter in their tasks; and tend, on the whole, to show evidence of good performance and achievement over a period of time (Atkinson & Feather, 1966; McClelland, 1961).

More recent extensions of achievement motivation ideas (Raynor, 1978) suggest that effective career striving on the part of achievement-oriented persons must involve a good deal of long-term planning. If a person's achievement motivation is to influence the quality of a particular performance, he or she must be aware of the relevance of that performance to long-term goals (Raynor, Atkinson, & Brown, 1974). This notion suggests that successful individuals should show a tendency to be highly aware of both future career paths and the instrumentality of particular courses of action for attaining these career advances. These people should also provide evidence of stability in their achievement strivings over a period of time. Given the greater obstacles they had to overcome, we expected that NPDs might exhibit even higher levels of need achievement than controls.

Atkinson (1958) also discussed two other motives: the need for affiliation and the need for power. As the need for affiliation (generally described as being motivated, in part, by a need to be near people), and the need for power (or being primarily concerned about gaining control over the means of influencing another) might be involved in the personal resources of successful women, it seems important to determine the relationship between these needs and paths of social mobility and career advancement. We expected that NPDs might have lower need for affiliation and higher need for power in order to overcome the negative affects of their family of origin.

Another influential factor in career decisions is the way in which the individual views potential costs or rewards. John Thibaut and Harold Kelley, writing in *The Social Psychology of Groups* (1959), suggested that it is sensible to distinguish between two personal orientations to the outcomes that may be available. Some people, they speculated, are particularly oriented toward the rewards they might obtain and relatively insensitive to the costs they might incur in the course of striving for those rewards. Such "reward-oriented" people were described by Thibaut and Kelley as tending to feel "confident, powerful, and oriented to success." In contrast, "cost-oriented" people, who are particularly sensitive to the costs they might suffer, were described as feeling generally "constricted, powerless, and oriented toward the avoidance of failure." As it would seem likely that those who attain unusual career accomplishments would tend to see opportunities in situations and to take action despite possible costs involved, it was expected that, in general, successful women would reflect a predisposition toward seeing potential rewards rather than costs. It seems plausible to expect NPD women to be even more reward oriented, again, to help them overcome the greater hurdles of family class and education. Another point of view, however, suggests that they might be allowed more cost orientation than usually associated with success because they had less to lose than controls. For this variable we perform truly exploratory research.

Two other personality variables of interest were locus of control and defenses against stress. Whereas people with an external locus of control believe that the most important causal influence for life events comes from uncontrollable external forces (i.e., the actions of others or luck), individuals with an internal locus of control believe that they themselves are the cause of most of the things that happen to them (Lefcourt, 1982; Rotter, 1966). For example, research relating locus of control to perceived outcomes has shown that individuals high in internal locus of control are better able to defer gratification for the promise of potentially larger reinforcements in the future (Kilpatrick, Durbin, & Marcotte, 1974). Lefcourt (1982) cited the cases from naturalistic sources of individuals in situations in which survival seems unlikely who persist in their efforts despite the unfavorable odds as being examples of belief in one's own ability to determine outcomes, or evidence of internal locus of control. It seems essential that NPD subjects would possess a strong sense of personal control over their life outcomes given that they had to overcome disadvantages stemming from their early backgrounds in order to attain success. This would not necessarily be true for controls, who, by accepting the potentially positive influence of the external forces associated with their lives (higher social class, etc.), could be aided in their striving for success. We therefore hypothesized that NPD women would exhibit a stronger internal locus of control than women who did not come from educationally and economically impoverished backgrounds. Related to this is the individual's orientation toward standards of performance. Shostrom (1965), for example, saw inner-directed people as creating and using their own standards of performance and conduct in judging their own and others' actions and work, whereas other-directed people are seen as seeking out and adopting the standards of others in judging the adequacy of their own and others' performances and outcomes. Thus the inner-directed person is autonomous, independent, and initiating. The other-directed person is more dependent on the standards of others and presumably more strongly oriented toward pleasing others and meeting their standards. Because successful women frequently have had to disregard conventional norms governing feminine social roles in order to achieve success, it was expected that, in general, these women would show evidence of adopting their own standards of evaluation.

The psychological literature on coping with stress, adversity, and conflict is large and particularly diverse; however, a number of researchers have focused on the relationship between positive life outcomes and the use of "mature" intrapsychic defenses such as altruism, humor, anticipation, and sublimation (Freud, 1937; Haan, 1964; Hartmann, 1958). Many psychologists believe this work on defenses is dated; however, the concept of "mature" defenses actually forms the theoretical basis of Erikson's notion of generativity (see Erikson, 1959), and defenses have been shown to be useful to the study of career success. The work on such preferred adaptive styles that is most closely relevant to our own interest is that of George Vaillant (1971, 1976, 1977). In 1967, Vaillant became associated with the Grant Study, a major longitudinal study of Harvard College undergraduates begun in 1937. Participants in the study were selected because they were deemed particularly promising, sound, stable young men. The more than 260 men so chosen were tested and interviewed extensively over a period of five years during their college years, and were then followed up periodically during the 30 years between their graduation and the mid 1970s.

For the purposes of this research, Vaillant (1977) classified ego-defense mechanisms into four levels. These are "Psychotic" (Level I), "Immature" (Level II), "Neurotic" (Level III), and "Mature" (Level IV). The mature defenses included altruism, humor, suppression, anticipation, and sublimation; the less mature mechanisms (Levels II and III) included such defenses as projection, intellectualization, and reaction formation. For example, altruism, briefly defined, involves vicarious but instinctually gratifying service to others; sublimation involves the indirect but constructive expression of instinctual needs. An individual using altruism to defend against dependency as a result of early parent-child interactions (or lack of interaction), might be actively involved in or donate large sums of money to foster care programs or rebuilding schools. The individual sublimating dependency needs, on the other hand, might end up in the teaching profession. Individuals utilizing "mature" defenses deal with instinctual needs in a constructive and sometimes creative way. Less mature defenses, however, frequently result in destructive outcomes for the individual. For example, the person who deals with dependency needs through reaction formation (that is, behaving in a diametrically opposed manner to instinctual needs) would be more likely to reject most forms of dependency and adopt an overly independent and potentially hostile orientation toward others.

What seems most striking about the results of Vaillant's study is that the preferred ego-defense mechanisms of the men in the sample discriminated to an astonishing degree between those whose life and career outcomes were particularly good and those whose career, interpersonal, and health outcomes were relatively poor. In his descriptions of the lives of people who exemplify his points about maturity of ego defenses, Vaillant (1977) implied that many of those whose defenses were judged to be in the mature category started life in relatively modest circumstances, and a number of the men who were socioeconomically advantaged during childhood did not develop productive styles of adaptation.

It stands to reason that successful individuals must have learned to deal with stress in a relatively constructive manner. We predict, therefore, that the predominant defensive styles would consist of defenses yielding constructive outcomes. For NPDs, however, two alternative expectations can be derived from the literature: (1) NPDs will have higher maturity defenses in light of the fact that it took "more" to get ahead; (2) given that defenses are patterned early in life, NPDs from economically and educationally disadvantaged backgrounds might have less mature defenses.

METHOD

In a multiyear exploratory study investigating the life history antecedents of extraordinary career success, 100 black and white men and women were extensively interviewed. The focus of the current report is the analysis of selected psychological and life history material for the women in the study. Other results have been reported elsewhere (Boardman & Harrington, 1984; Harrington, in preparation).

The present sample consists of 25 black and 24 white women between the ages of 40 and 55 who had achieved often extraordinary levels of occupational success in business, academia, or government service. The sample includes managers and entrepreneurs in commerce and industry; members of high-status service professions such as lawyers and university professors; basic and applied researchers; and high-level local, state, and national political figures. The age range chosen recognizes that many women, because of their additional role responsibilities (see Rossi, 1985), tend to reach midcareer somewhat later than men; some women have begun careers after discharging obligations they have felt as mothers of infants and young children, and others have sustained career interruptions for similar reasons. Of these women, 29 were negative prediction defiers, operationalized as those who grew up in low socioeconomic status families where neither parent had completed high school. A control group consisted of 20 individuals who achieved comparable occupational success coming from middle-class to upper-middle-class backgrounds with parents who were at least high school graduates. Definitions of the respondents' original socioeconomic status were defined by local community standards. (For example, one woman was referred who grew up in Appalachia. However, when it was discovered that she was the daughter of a local store owner, she was excluded from consideration as a negative prediction defier. Her position in the community would have been middle class by local standards.)

Subjects were selected for the study through the use of social networks (to form a sample of opportunity) enlarged through a "snowball" procedure in which subjects nominated future subjects. This was constrained by the criterion that no more than two subjects would come from any one source in each of the occupational groups selected. Success was peer defined; that is, a career was seen as being unusually successful if it were so considered by "experts" already established in that field. Judgments of success were not affected by origin data. Levels of success for both NPD and control subjects were comparable.

When the prospective respondent was contacted, the purpose of the research was fully explained and the general nature of the interview was described. The interview was conducted in a private place chosen by the respondent, where she felt comfortable discussing autobiographical material—perhaps in the respondent's home—or an equally comfortable and private place provided by the interviewing team. The respondent was assured of the total confidentiality of the interview, and the means chosen to protect that confidentiality were explained.

The taped life history interview, approximately three to four hours in length, was conducted by a team of two individuals, at least one of whom was of the same sex and race as the respondent. The interview covered such areas as employment history, schooling, family of orgin, current family, health, and general summary questions involving success attributions, friendship patterns, and overall satisfactions with personal life and career.

As previously discussed, two classes of variables were of particular interest in the collection and analysis of the data. Those reported here include particular psychological characteristics of the respondent (e.g., level of achievement motivation, reward-cost orientation, internal-external locus of control, power and affiliation needs, and strategies for coping with stress and conflict) and certain life history variables (e.g., family and career networks, support systems, and level of personal/professional satisfaction) which enabled these people to achieve success.

Analysis of the data involved several steps. Interview tapes were first transcribed and then a content analysis was conducted. Using a 5-point coding scheme that ranged from "absent" to "strong," the tapes (in conjunction with the transcriptions) were coded for the presence of the aforementioned psychological themes to determine the relationship of these themes to paths of social mobility and career advancement. Judgments were made on the following basis: If evidence of the psychological theme (as reflected in particular phrases, philosophies, and styles of coping) was pervasive in the subjects' life, characterizing many of their thoughts, responses, and approaches, it was coded as being strong. If the theme was present, characterizing strong responses and approaches but not pervasive in the subjects' life, it was coded as being more moderate in strength. Weaker ratings were given in instances in which the psychological theme was present in only a few responses and approaches; otherwise, it was given an "absent" rating. Coding was conducted by social and clinical psychologists and psychological anthropologists trained over a period of weeks. Intercoder reliability ranged from .79 to 1.00. Median splits were used to do the analyses reported here.

RESULTS AND DISCUSSION

Profile of the Successful Woman

Despite the extremely different backgrounds of the women in this study, we discovered a striking similarity among them with respect to many of the aforementioned personality characteristics. For example, 94% of those interviewed were rated as being moderate or strong in need for achievement. These individuals consistently reflect a concern for standards of excellence and good performance. For example, one university president described her graduate school and early job experience as follows:

The combination of the course work and the research assistantship was a superb training; by the time I finished my graduate work I had the equivalent in articles of a book. . . . They offered me a job as an assistant professor which was unheard of. They did not hire their own. . . . I published more than the entire department together in one year.

Another woman administrator expressed her concern with excellence through her research efforts:

Right now I'm making a strong push to spend less time in administrative work and more time doing research. I think ultimately I might have more to contribute there. . . . I'd love to be able to say something clearer about [names her research area]. I'd like to be able to show how these factors interact. I'd like to eventually write a book dealing with this. I'd also like to write a textbook.

However, with respect to need for power and need for affiliation themes, these successful women were split: 53% were rated as being moderate or strong and 47% were rated as being weak or absent for nPower; 55% were moderate or strong in affiliation needs, whereas 45% were rated as being weak or absent.

Furthermore, women in the sample were judged to be primarily reward-oriented and inner-directed and to have an internal locus of control. Specifically, 74% were judged to be reward-oriented versus 26% who were judged to be predominantly cost-oriented. For example, one black woman natural scientist, judged to be predominantly reward-oriented, described the initial step she took toward going to graduate school:

I had written to many people that I considered to be important in the scientific community. I did not know them. And the person was a doctor. . . . He was important and he had written all these books. I wrote to him and told him all about myself and that I wanted to go to graduate school and I didn't know how. And the man wrote me back, told me who to go see in New York. I did.

This, of course, is another example of how a psychological variable—in this case putting oneself at risk—interacts with nonreplicable serendipitous events: not only did he respond, he became a sponsor of her career.

Concerning the internal-external dimension, 67% were judged to
have an internal locus of control as compared to 33% who were judged
to have predominantly an external locus of control. For the ability to
define one's own standards, 80% were judged to be inner-directed.
Only 20% were predominantly other-directed. Furthermore, the
defense mechanisms used were most often those associated with
constructive outcomes in life: intellectualization, altruism, suppression, humor, and sublimation. In fact, 80% used *only* constructive
defenses in dealing with stress and conflicts.

One final note: Success also had its associated costs; 80% of the
subjects showed evidence of incurring costs in the areas of family and
intimate relationships, leisure time, and health—with the most
frequently occurring costs involving family and intimate relationships and leisure time. As one successful scientist put it,

> I think it's a problem for any single female who's over 41 years old. I
> really do. In terms of my own personal social life, it's been very costful.
> I still am not clear about how to deal with all of this. . . . Any fairly
> successful, assertive, secure woman has got some more problems in
> today's society. Finding an interesting man who's at least equally
> successful, equally secure, who's not threatened by what I am and what
> I do, with whom I'm able to have a personal and academic and
> intellectual interchange on equal footing. I don't find many of these
> people.

In contrast, it is interesting to note that only 50% of the men in the
larger sample showed evidence of such costs (Harrington, in
preparation).

NPD/Control Differences

Although these factors characterizing successful women in general
are interesting, the main thrust of our analyses was to find the
differences between NPD and control subjects as well as to explore
whatever differences exist between black and white subjects. When-
ever appropriate, two-way analyses of variance were conducted on the
dependent variables of interest; in other cases the chi-square test of
association was computed to examine differences between the groups
on either status or race.

In analyzing the differences between NPDs and controls, two main themes emerge, one psychological and the other concerning career patterns. Psychologically, NPDs have an unusually strong belief in their ability to control what goes on in their lives. As hypothesized, NPDs were significantly higher than controls in internal locus of control, $F(1,48) = 4.06$, $p < .05$.

A number of studies have shown that this belief in personal control has a positive effect upon performance, affect, and even health (Langer & Benevento, 1978; Rotter, 1966; Wortman & Brehm, 1975). In a related area Antonovsky (1983), investigating the concept of a "sense of coherence" (belief that life events were predictable), found that those with a strong sense of coherence view events in life as experiences to be coped with and challenges to be met. It seems likely that a strong sense of personal control played a major role in the achievement of success of NPDs who initially had more to overcome than controls. This sense of personal control is clearly reflected in their orientation toward work. As one said,

> Over the long haul I think you do your own thing wherever you are, and really it's up to you. If you're going to do significant writing and if you're going to do some research or if you're going to develop your mind in some important way, you're going to do that wherever you are."

In a similar vein another said,

> I worked very hard. I feel that I made myself . . . but I feel I would have made a success of myself even if I hadn't gone this route. . . . I would have been doing something that people would have noticed. I was determined to fulfill myself.

Still another woman expressed her sense of personal control with the following: "You can do anything if you put your mind to it. It may take a long time, but if you put your mind to it, you'll do it."

Related to this, NPDs were found to be significantly *lower* in reward orientation than controls (see Table 5.1). The lower reward orientation is consistent with an internal locus of control, given that many rewards are external. The lower reward orientation shown by NPDs relative to controls may be a result of a more realistic assessment of the greater difficulties involved for NPDs in attaining

Table 5.1
Summary Table—Origin Differences

	Origin	
Variable	NPD (n = 29)	Control (n = 20)
Reward orientation		
High	7	12
Moderate or less	22	8
χ^2 (1, n = 49) = 4.99, $p < .05$.		
Altruism		
High	9	2
Moderate or less	6	10
χ^2 (1, n = 27) = 3.55, p < .06.		
Frequency of mentioning contact with people at work as motivating force		
No mention contact	19	19
Mention contact	10	1
χ^2 (1, n = 49) = 4.34, $p < .05$.		
Frequency of mentioning friends from work as part of social network		
No mention friends	17	18
Mention friends	12	2
χ^2 (1, n = 49) = 4.28, p < .05.		

Note. 14 NPD subjects and 8 controls were not coded for altruism.

career success. Coming from a background in which external reward would not be as salient, NPDs' belief in personal control coupled with an absence of rewards in early life seem to reinforce their self-sufficiency. In fact, a post hoc analysis revealed a trend that individuals who were high in internal locus of control were less likely to be reward-oriented than those who were low in internal locus of control.

Being sensitive to what it takes to get ahead as well as the costs associated with upward mobility, NPDs also appear to be more willing to help others get ahead than do controls. NPDs tended to use altruism to a greater extent than controls. This was the only difference between the two groups when the data on defense mechanisms was examined. No significant differences were found between NPDs and controls for need achievement, affiliation, or power motives.

The second theme reflects the *costs* incurred by negative prediction defiers in attaining success. As with the total sample, NPDs experi-

enced costs as well as success; however, *twice* as many NPDs as
controls reported costs associated with their occupational position.
One major cost for these women involved the loss of a sense of
continuity. Although it may seem to some that success is its own
reward, upward mobility also brings a psychologically stressful
disruption of early friendships, home, and community (Stacey, 1967).
For example, NPDs more often mentioned feeling unable to relate to
people associated with their early lives. In describing a recent reunion
with two of her college girlfriends, one scientist said:

> They married their high school sweethearts . . . they took many years
> out to raise kids and they're both going back to teaching full time but
> have no tenure. . . . I'm the only woman with a doctoral degree that
> these two women know at all. . . . on the one hand we're the same as we
> were before, on the other hand we are light years apart from one
> another. If I'd . . . stayed [in my home area] I might have married [my
> high school sweetheart] and become a fifth-grade school teacher for the
> rest of my life.

This disruption of identity with early support systems may
account for the trend we found for black women to be less reward
oriented than white women, $F(1,48) = 3.87$, $p < .06$ In addition, we
found that black women were significantly less likely to leave their
NPDs were significantly more likely to report contact with people as
a motivating force in their decisions about careers. In fact, over
one-third of all NPDs report this as a major satisfaction for them, in
contrast to only one control who mentioned this feature of the work
environment as being important. NPDs also cited friends from work
as being an important part of their social network significantly more
often than did women from more affluent backgrounds.

Ethnic Differences

With respect to black/white differences, it was felt that the
difficulties female NPDs have faced would most likely have been
intensified for black females. Black NPDs have often had to deal with
racism as well as the obstacles of sexism and family of origin. Several
of the previously discussed differences found between NPDs and
controls were in fact influenced by race. For instance, it was the black

NPDs who were significantly more likely to cite the importance of friends from work in their lives. Although this pattern also occurred with white NPDs, it did not reach significance for that group alone.

Use of the defense mechanism of altruism was also influenced by race (see Table 5.2). Black NPDs were significantly higher in the use of altruism as a way to cope with conflict and stress than were either black controls or white subjects. For example, one black woman currently holding political office spoke of fighting for and gaining better working conditions as being a fulfilling part of her work. Another black woman physician described her intense involvement in community affairs and the development of a community health clinic:

> We had community meetings, whether they were big ones or small ones it didn't matter. The thing that mattered to me was to really listen to what people said they felt they needed. . . . It was really like educating your community on issues like health care . . . if you got sick you had hospitals, period. Poor people had no where else to go . . . and we kept saying there must be another way. Why must people suffer because they cannot get health care? . . . We came up with the idea of having a free neighborhood clinic, and a year later we opened with a group of volunteers.

The fact that black NPDs use altruism more than black controls and white subjects may be due to their intensified circumstantial victimization. Whereas having experienced victimization themselves has fostered in these subjects an increased compassion for others, it most likely has also increased their awareness of the difficulties involved in attaining success. This awareness of "what it takes" most likely accounts for the significant tendency of black subjects to attribute their successful positions to ability rather than to luck or having received help from other people.

Realization of the achievement effort and ability required for success combined with awareness of the difficulties involved may also account for the trend we found for black women to be less reward oriented than white women, $F(1, 48) = 3.87, p > .06$. In addition, we found that black women were significantly less likely to leave their jobs because of salary than were white women. This is consistent with the idea that something other than monetary or other tangible rewards has become most satisfying to them. This was the single

Table 5.2
Summary Table—Differences Within Black Subjects

	Origin	
Variable	NPD (n = 15)	Control (n = 10)
Frequency of mentioning friends from work as part of social network		
No mention work friends	6	9
Mention work friends	9	1
χ^2 (1, n = 25) = 4.34, p < .05.		
Altruism		
Strong	7	1
Moderate or less	3	7
Fisher exact probability test, p < .05.		

Note. 5 NPD subjects and 2 controls were not coded for altruism.

Table 5.3
Summary Table—Black/White Differences

	Race	
Variable	Black (n = 25)	White (n = 24)
Frequency of explaining success as being due to ability		
No mention ability	17	23
Mention ability	8	1
χ^2 (1, n = 49) = 4.61, p < .05.		
Frequency of mentioning higher salary as reason for job change		
No mention salary	23	14
Mention salary	2	10
χ^2 (1, n = 49) = 5.80, p < .05.		

significant difference between black and white women involving reasons for having made major job changes.

CONCLUSIONS

This chapter is addressed to an important but narrow problem: How do successful women (aged 40-55) who come from educationally and economically disadvantaged backgrounds differ psychologically from equally successful women who grew up in more advantaged circumstances? We found that the two cohorts had much in common but also some important differences that should guide future research and eventually practice.

Despite the different backgrounds, the women of our study shared many personality characteristics. They were high in our measures of need achievement, mature in their defenses, and predominantly reward-oriented, inner-directed, and internal rather than external in their locus of control. Also, in contrast to men in the larger study, they were more likely to report that their success had come at some cost, usually in the areas of family or personal relationships. On the whole, these successful people exhibited traits that we have come to associate with psychological wellness, a sense of self and coherence.

The main focus of our study, however, was to identify points of difference between the two cohorts to see what, if anything, distinguished successful women who had come from fundamentally different origins. Our initial impetus to this research came about from the existence, within the Institute for Urban and Minority Education which Harrington directs, of several projects designed to be of assistance to educationally and economically disadvantaged children. We found a dearth of literature about how people, particularly women and blacks, from such backgrounds actually construct successful careers. In other words, what real-life compensations do such people make? We decided that the open-ended study of life histories described here was a way to begin to find out.

We believe the most important difference between the two groups was the significantly more internal locus of control of the NPD cohort. Given the environments in which these women were born, the belief that one could still exert control over one's fate and not have to give in to external forces must be quite important. For the more advantaged group, however, an external locus of control in and of itself would not necessarily be limiting. One may succeed simply by following the path of least resistance. But for the daughter of a sharecropper walking five miles to school each day such fatalism might become, from a career point of view, fatal.

The finding that NPD women are lower in reward orientation than controls is linked partly to this internal locus of control (with which it is correlated in our study) and partly to a range of variables described next. The NPD women may be more cost-conscious because of their origins, and they may seek rewards less because of their extreme internality of control, which makes external rewards less salient. However, this finding is also linked to another set of findings that suggest powerful career differences between NPDs and controls. NPDs, by being more altruistic and willing to help others, despite the absence of difference on variables like nPower and nAffiliation (black controls had higher nAffiliation than the black NPDs or white controls, which indicates they were more aware of belonging to an unusual tradition) and by being more likely to report costs (again particularly relational) of success, become more likely to rely on work and career as the source of interpersonal support. They are more likely to report contact with people as a motivating force in their decisions about careers and as a source of satisfaction in their lives. Their friendship networks come from work, and this means that even their pay is work-linked. This constellation of variables—altruism toward fellow employees, reliance on work for formation of personal friends and support networks, and an overall blurring of distinctions between personal and business relationships—would appear to have profound implications for what expectations these women have of work and what work may reasonably demand of them. It seems especially likely that they will wind up devoting more time to their work than do controls, which may not be incidental to their overall success, however neurotic some may find their motives for their devotion. In this way one of the costs of success—the disruption of early friendships and continuity with the past—becomes an asset as it directs more and more energy toward work and the people with whom one works.

The research reported here, if supported by further research, has implications for many fields. In education, for example, it suggests that variables not necessarily conducive to good classroom control—such as an internal locus of control, openness to opportunity, and risk taking—may be critical to later life success. To researchers in careers it suggests that a diversity of psychological traits may lead to similar outcomes (i.e., success). It also suggests that companies that consciously would like to encourage women, blacks, and other disadvantaged populations should not assume that what makes these people become successful is no different from what makes anyone successful. The fact that the differences reported above between NPDs and controls were almost always even stronger for the black NPDs should not be overlooked.

REFERENCES

Antonovsky, A. (1983, March). The sense of ~oherence: Development of a research instrument. *Newsletter and Research Reports, 1,* 11-22.

Atkinson, J. W. (Ed.). (1958). *Motives in fantasy, action, and society: A method of assessment and study.* Princeton: Van Nostrand.

Atkinson, J. W., & Feather, N. T. (Eds.). (1966). *A theory of achievement motivation.* New York: John Wiley.

Boardman, S. K., & Harrington, C. C. (1984, August). Strategies for career success. In L. L. Moore (Chair), *Paths for women to the corporate fast track.* Symposium conducted at the conference on Women and Organizations, Simmons College, Boston.

Erikson, E. (1959). Identity and the life cycle. *Psychological Issues, 1,* 18-64.

Freud, A. (1937). *Ego and the mechanisms of defense.* London: Hogarth Press.

Goertzel, M. V., & Goertzel, T. (1978). *Three hundred eminent personalities.* San Francisco: Jossey-Bass.

Haan, N. (1964). The relationship of ego functioning and intelligence to social status and mobility. *Journal of Abnormal and Social Psychology, 69,* 594-605.

Harrington, C. C. (in preparation). *Pathways to success: Antecedents and consequences of extraordinary mobility in American men and women.* Final Report to the Spencer Foundation, Teachers College, Columbia University.

Hartmann, H. (1958). *Ego psychology and the problem of adaptation.* New York: International Universities Press.

Kilpatrick, D. G., Durbin, W. R., & Marcotte, D. B. (1974). Personality, stress of the medical education process, and change in affective mood state. *Psychological Reports, 34,* 1215-1223.

Langer, E. J., & Benevento, A. (1978). Self-induced dependence. *Journal of Personality and Social Psychology, 36,* 886-893.

Lefcourt, H. M. (1982). *Locus of control* (2nd ed.) Hillsdale, NJ: Lawrence Erlbaum.

Levinson, D. J., Darrow, C. N., Klein, E. B., Levinson, M. H. & McKee, B. (1978). *The seasons of a man's life.* New York: Ballentine Books.

McClelland, D. C. (1961). *The achieving society.* New York: Van Nostrand.

Nieva, V. F., & Gutek, B. A. (1981). *Women and work.* New York: Praeger.

Raynor, J. O. (1978). Motivation and career striving. In J. W. Atkinson & J. O. Raynor (eds.), *Personality, motivation and achievement.* Washington, DC: Hemisphere.

Raynor, J. O., Atkinson, J. W., & Brown, M. (1974). Subjective aspects of achievement motivation immediately before and examination. In J. W. Atkinson & J. O. Raynor (Eds.) *Personality, motivation and achievement.* Washington, DC: Hemisphere.

Rossi, A. S. (Ed.). (1985). *Gender and the life course.* New York: Aldine.

Rotter, J. B. (1966). Generalized expectancies for internal versus external control of reinforcement. *Psychological Monographs, 80*(1), (Whole No. 609).

Shostrom, E. L. (1965). A test for the measurement of self-actualization. *Educational and Psychological Measurement, 24,* 207-218.

Stacey, B. (1967). Some psychological consequences of inter-generational mobility. *Human relations, 20,* 3-12.

Thibaut, J. W., & Kelley, H. H. (1959). *The social psychology of groups*. New York: John Wiley.

Vaillant, G. E. (1971). Theoretical hierarchy of adaptive ego mechanisms. *Archives of General Psychiatry, 24,* 107-118.

Vaillant, G. E. (1976). Natural history of male psychological health: The relation of choice to ego mechanisms of defense to adult adjustment. *Archives of General Psychiatry, 33,* 535-545.

Vaillant, G. E. (1977). *Adaptation to life*. Boston: Little, Brown.

Wortman, C. B., & Brehm, J. W. (1975). Responses to uncontrollable outcomes: An integration of reactance theory and the learned helplessness model. In L. Berkowitz (Ed.), *Advances in experimental social psychology* (Vol. 8, pp. 277-336). New York: Academic Press.

6

Appraising the Performance of Women
Gender and the Naval Officer

PATRICIA J. THOMAS

In laboratory experiments performance attributed to a woman generally is rated lower than identical performance attributed to a man. Because appraisals of job performance play such a crucial role in career development, a research study was undertaken to investigate whether gender influences judgments of the job behavior of real people. A content analysis was conducted of the narrative section of the evaluations of 239 naval officers. The number and nature of descriptors applied to each gender were tallied and tested for significance. In addition, cluster and discriminate analyses were performed on the personality traits appearing in the evaluations to investigate sex-role stereotyping. Finally, two composite narratives were created of words typically used to describe a female or a male officer, leaving out all reference to gender. Mid-level Navy officers were asked to review these two evaluations and recommend only one of the "officers" for promotion. The findings indicate that men's evaluations are more career enhancing than women's.

In the organizational environment, performance evaluations serve several purposes. For individuals, they reveal supervisory judgments concerning job-related strengths and weaknesses and provide the insight needed to improve performance. They are a mechanism by

---

Author's Note: The opinions expressed in this chapter are those of the author and not official and do not necessarily reflect the views of the Navy Department.

which an individual's career progress is assessed. For management, they promote organizational goals by identifying talented personnel worthy of development, encouragement, and advancement. Brinker-hoff and Kanter (1980) posit that performance appraisal is a tool in the organizational control process used to channel the behavior of employees and justify decisions made about their assignments and tenure.

To satisfy organizational and individual needs, appraisals must reflect "true performance" with reasonable accuracy. Numerous researchers, however, have demonstrated that evaluations of job performance fall far short of this goal, suffering from halo effect, inflation, and low interrater reliability and yielding different results when the purpose for the evaluation is varied. In addition to process and psychometric problems, personal factors cannot be discounted. As Zedeck and Cascio (1984) point out, appraisal is not simply a judgment of job behavior based on objective components but involves filtering information through the social cognitive structure of the ratee. Thus the outcome is affected by liking for the ratee (Cardy & Dobbins, 1984), preconceptions about the individual's performance (Webster & Driskell, 1978), and acquisition of relevant knowledge about the ratee (DeNisi, Cafferty, & Meglino, 1984), to name a few of the variables that have been identified. Status characteristics, such as rank, race, gender, education, and age also influence appraisals, particularly when the rater and ratee are not well acquainted.

Gender, of course, has a powerful influence on interactions on and off the job. In the context of evaluation, knowledge of gender consistently has been shown to have a significant effect on the dependent variable, be it resumé, work of art, writing, or videotape of task performance. Nieva and Gutek (1981) reviewed 24 studies that investigated the effect of gender on evaluation: four showed no bias; four showed pro-female bias, and 16 showed pro-male bias. Explaining these results solely on the basis of gender is simplistic, of course. Among the variables shown to moderate the outcome are sex-appropriateness of the task or work behavior (Rosen & Jerdee, 1973; Isaacs, 1981), status of the performer (Wiley & Eskilson, 1982), level of competence of the performer (Deaux & Taynor, 1973; Bigoness, 1976), vagueness of the evaluation criteria (Lenney, Mitchell, & Browning, 1983), quantity of data on which to base the evaluation (Frank & Drucker, 1977), and sex of subjects (Palundi & Strayer, 1985). Nevertheless, the majority of studies yielded results indicating that performance attributed to a woman is devalued in comparison to identical performance attributed to a man. Although all of these studies were conducted on protocols, the need to determine whether the performance evaluations of real women and men differ is apparent because of the potential impact on women's careers. Such an investigation was undertaken among comissioned line officers of the U.S. Navy and is the subject of this chapter.

EVALUATION OF THE PERFORMANCE
OF NAVY OFFICERS

Performance appraisal of military officers differs from that of civilian managers in several ways. First, officers are geographically mobile and very numerous. While the first draft of their evaluations is prepared by an immediate superior, it is "written" by the commanding officer for people who are unacquainted with the officer yet must make critical personnel decisions about her/his career (i.e., promotion, transfer, special assignment, separation). Second, officers are educated, dedicated, and well-trained so motivation and discipline need not be a goal of the evaluation system. Third, potential, not just past performance, is a vital part of military evaluations—some would say the most important function of the appraisal process. Future value to the organization is usually indicated by the rater through an enumeration of relevant personality traits, a discussion of outstanding performance during the rating period, and recommendations for career-enhancing assignments.

The military is a closed system in that all openings are filled from within. This fact, along with an "up or out" policy,[1] promotes inflation of quantitative and qualitative judgments appearing in appraisals. In the narrative portion of evaluations, inflation results in common words losing their usual meanings and a proliferation of officers who all but walk on water. Admiral Elmo Zumwalt once discussed the disservice paid an officer by a well-intentioned civilian who described his subordinate as an "excellent officer." To those initiated in the language of military evaluations and people deciding the fate of that officer, "excellent" means "adequate."

Navy officers are evaluated using the Report on the Fitness of Officers, commonly called the FitRep. This form requires that reporting seniors assign ratings and rankings to specific aspects of performance, specialty skills, contributions to the command's mission, and certain personal traits. The final item asks raters to write comments on the officer's overall leadership ability, personal traits not listed in the rating blocks, estimated or actual performance in combat, and unique skills and distinctions that may be important to career development and future assignments. The form is revised periodically to reflect the changing emphasis in officer development and halt temporarily the seemingly inevitable inflation that familiarity with a rating form breeds. Yet, as Haering (1980) noted,

> It doesn't take long for the grades to cluster around the high left end again. . . . The way selection or screening boards learn to live with this apparent and uniform pattern of excellence is reliance upon service reputation and, if that fails, by a search for nuances, oddities, and subtleties. These may tell a story which separates the promising officer from the merely diligent one. (p. 35)

Thus although the Fitness Report requires quantitative judgments on scales intended to be objective, critical decisions about the careers of naval officers are often based on qualitative, subjective material. Such material is vulnerable to the influence of personal biases and stereotypes, particularly when personality traits are being discussed. Moreover, there is no assurance that a well-written, unbiased evaluation will be interpreted without regard to gender, race, ethnicity, and so on when the task of the reader is to infer the significance of subtleties.

Navy officers who happen to be women are at a disadvantage in that they are not as useful to the military as are men. This does not imply that they are not as useful in their particular assignments or are deficient in any way—only that they cannot be used in the full range of military jobs due to 10 U.S.C., Section 6015.[2] This law results in women not being groomed throughout their careers for operational positions, as men are, because they cannot command a surface or subsurface ship, an aviation squadron, or any other activity for which operational experience is a prerequisite. Senior officers, who prepare evaluations with the interests of the Navy in mind, strive to make their subordinates who possess "the right stuff" competitive with others of their rank. If that subordinate is female, however, her performance evaluation may consciously or unconsciously reflect the reality of women's role in an effective military organization.

Until the passage of the Defense Officer Personnel Management Act in September 1981, gender differences in FitReps were of little consequence because separate selection boards were convened to consider the records of female and male officers. Since that time, however, women have been in competition with men for promotions despite policies that prohibit them from holding many assignments vital to the Navy's mission. To counter the effect of these policies, the Secretary of the Navy, in his precept to selection boards, reminds the members that gender *should* be taken into consideration when assessing career experiences. He further instructs the boards to focus on performance in making their selections. Although the intent of such guidance cannot be faulted, it poses a hidden danger if the work behavior of women and men is evaluated differently.

The Navy has strong injunctions against bias and routinely monitors various personnel systems to ensure that people are being treated equitably. As part of this effort, quantitative rankings and marks assigned to female and male officers have been monitored for several years and do not differ significantly. Narrative material is not reviewed, however, even though the vulnerability of personality traits to stereotyping is well documented. Broverman, Vogel, Broverman, Clarkson, and Rosenkrantz (1972) identified 29 traits associated with typical male behavior and 12 with typical female behavior. The masculine traits formed a "competency" cluster, which consisted of such descriptors as aggressive, independent, competitive, logical, and decisive. The feminine traits formed a "warmth-expressiveness" cluster, which consisted of such descriptors as talkative, tactful, expressive of feelings, and gentle. Although both clusters have a positive effect, most employers value competency more highly than expressiveness, and the military, in particular, values masculine traits. Even if women display competency and assertiveness, they may find that in the eyes of their superiors they are women first and naval officers second. Moreover, being described in masculine terms has its attendant risks. Costrich, Feinstein, Kidder, Maracek, and Pascale (1975) studied the social consequences of women behaving in an assertive, aggressive mode and men behaving in a passive, dependent manner. The results indicated that when members of either sex deviate from expected behavioral norms, they are viewed as being unlikable and in poor psychological health.

The review of the literature and the organizational emphasis of the military suggests that women naval officers are prime candidates for differential evaluation. As Nieva and Gutek (1981) pointed out, "sex-related bias presents the greatest problem for successful or competent women in situations where there is considerable ambiguity, and which involve sex-inappropriate situations or require sex-role-incongruent behaviors" (p. 81). The narrative material (ambiguous) in the Fitness Reports of women line officers (sex-role incongruous) who are in zone for promotion to lieutenant commander (successful and competent) fulfills all three of these conditions.

EXPERIMENTAL PROCEDURE

A research study was conducted in 1983 to determine whether female and male Navy officers are evaluated without regard to gender. The hypotheses that were developed addressed equity in evaluation and the presence of sex-role stereotyping. These hypotheses were as follows:

Hypothesis 1: There will be no difference in the *number* of personality traits described for women and men. However, the traits associated with a female officer will differ from those associated with a male officer.

Hypothesis 2: There will be no difference in the number or nature of descriptions of job-related skills, professional performance, or recommendations in women's and men's evaluations.

Hypothesis 3: Leadership skills will be mentioned more frequently in men's narratives than in women's; management/administrative skills will be mentioned more frequently in women's narratives.

The sample was obtained from the cohort of unrestricted line (URL) officers in year-groups 1972-1974 who were being considered for promotion to lieutenant commander in April 1981. Thus these officers were matched on time in the Navy and organizational function. They were the last group of lieutenants to be selected for promotion from gender-segregated lists of eligibles.

All FitReps completed during an officer's career are available to selection boards on a single microfiche. These microfiches were obtained for the 239 (120 women, 119 men) members of the sample. The FitReps selected for analysis represented the most recent, regular (as opposed to special) evaluation based on close observation of the ratee over a period of six or more months. Also, prior FitReps for the first 50 sample members on the roster were selected for use in the content analysis.

Content Analysis

To conduct a content analysis, units of information in narrative material must be identified and coded for later statistical analysis. As this process is somewhat subjective, objectivity is increased by developing rules for compiling and utilizing the list of descriptors, practicing on additional material to resolve differences between judges, and refining and enlarging the list as unique information is encountered. This process continues until a satisfactory level of interrater reliability is achieved (.80 or higher) and unique descriptors are no longer found. Then the actual narrative material to be analyzed is unitized and coded independently by at least two researchers.

In the evaluations of officers, seven categories of information were anticipated based on the instructions for completing Section 88 of the FitRep (BUPERSINST 1611.12E): manner of performance, personality traits, self-expression, combat performance (estimated or actual), impact on Navy/command, and recommendations (for promotion or future assignment). Content analyses of 10 of the extra 50 FitReps disclosed that two additional categories were needed: relations with others and Navy variables (associated with the naval officer role). In addition, the leadership category was expanded to include management and administrative skills.

The descriptors found in the 10 FitReps that were content analyzed were listed and assigned a code for a preliminary check on the ability of the research assistants to recognize the descriptor units and adjust to the rules. The major rules are as follows:

(1) A descriptor can describe how work is performed but not the work itself.
(2) When a statement contains more than one descriptor, whether a single word, phrase, or sentence, all should be counted.
(3) Descriptors that are repeated are counted only once.

Twenty of the remaining extra FitReps were content analyzed to amplify the list of descriptors (the remaining FitReps were not used) and provide practice for the two assistants who would be analyzing the actual data. Based on the additional information from these FitReps, synonymous words or phrases were combined for the list of descriptors.[3] In addition, the assistants' reliability in recognizing and coding units of information was checked using the following formula, taken from Guetzkow (1950), to determine consistency (U) in identifying units:

$$U = \frac{0_1 - 0_2}{0_1 + 0_2},$$

where 0_1 and 0_2 are the number of units identified by coders 1 and 2, respectively. Unlike traditional reliability coefficients, the smaller the value of U, the greater the accuracy of the coders. Scott's (1955) index of intercoder agreement (π) was used to determine content reliability:

$$\pi = \frac{P_o - P_e}{1 - P_e},$$

where P_o and P_e are the observed and expected percentages of agreement, respectively.

The final list of information categories and component descriptors is presented in Table 6.1.

Statistical Analyses

A list of descriptors (i.e., coded units) was compiled for each person in the sample. These lists were analyzed to investigate the hypotheses as follows:

Hypothesis 1. A t-test for the difference between means was computed to determine whether the same number of descriptors was used to describe the personality traits of women and men. A direct (as opposed to stepwise) discriminant analysis investigated the power of

Table 6.1

Coded Information Categories and Component Descriptors

Category/Descriptors	Category/Descriptors	Category/Descriptors
100 Manner of Performance 101 Outstanding performer 102 Competent/knowledgeable 103 Accomplished goals 104 Exercised sound judgment 105 Effective/productive 106 Professional 107 Completed tasks ahead of time 108 Contributed meaningfully 109 Showed satisfactory growth 110 Praiseworthy *200 Personality Traits* 200 Intelligent 202 Thorough 203 Organized/sets priorities 204 Flexible 205 Motivated/dedicated 206 Dependable/responsible 207 Displays initiative 208 Perceptive 209 Prompt 210 Logical/displays common sense 211 Honest 212 Dynamic 213 Sociable/good-natured 214 Energetic 215 Assertive/persuasive 216 Mature/stable 217 Confident 218 Creative 219 Aggressive 220 Positive/optimistic 221 Tactful	*300 Relations with Others* 301 Instructive 302 Attentive to needs of others 303 Unbiased/fair 304 Assists others 305 Displays good counseling skills 306 Demanding 307 Developmental 308 Displays team-building skills 309 Motivating *400 Self-Expression* 401 Written 402 Oral 403 Command of language *500 Combat Performance* 501 Would perform capably *600 Recommendations (For Promotion* *or Future Assignment)* 601 Shows potential for growth 602 Shows unlimited potential 603 Recom. for promotion ahead of contemporaries 604 Ready for LCDR/increased responsibility 605 Recom. for specific assignment 606 Recom. for demanding assignment 607 Recom. for immediate promotion 608 Highly recom. for promotion	*700 Navy Variables* 701 Possesses Navy characteristics 702 Follows rules/supports policies 703 Keeps physically fit 704 Well-groomed 705 Safety conscious 706 Valuable asset 707 Has supportive spouse 708 Active in community 709 Active in Navy social events, functions 710 Actively supports equal opportunity programs 711 Displays military bearing 712 Enhances camaraderie 713 Enhances national or international relations *800 Leadership and Management/Administration* 801 Capable leader 802 Capable manager/administrator *900 Impact on Navy/Command* 901 On unit readiness 902 On performance of wing, ship, command 903 On retention 904 On savings of time, money 905 On recruiting 906 On equal opportunity 907 On special programs 908 On material facilities/environment 909 On inspection conditions 910 On safety 911 On systems 912 On training

these traits to differentiate between the sexes. In addition, a separate single-linkage cluster analysis identified the patterns of traits clustering together for female and male officers.

Hypothesis 2. The means determined for the manner of performance, relations with others, self-expression, combat performance, recommendations, Navy variables, and impact on Navy/command categories were tested for gender differences with a two-tailed t-test. The number of times that each descriptor in these categories was used in the narrative evaluations of women and men was compared.

Hypothesis 3. The frequency of comments about leadership and management/administrative skills was compared for women and men using the z-ratio for the difference between proportions.

Determining the Practical Implications

In addition to the content and statistical analyses, a third type of data treatment was planned *if* differences between the sexes were found. The logical response to an investigation of potential bias is, "Does it matter in real-world terms?" Thus in an attempt to answer this question, two pseudo-FitRep narratives would be developed—one typifying a female officer and the other a male officer—without using any pronouns that denote gender. These FitRep narratives would be given to a group of naval officers, LCDR and above, to determine whether one enhanced promotional opportunities more than the other. They would be developed according to two rules. First, descriptors found in the significance tests or discriminant analysis to be associated with one sex more than the other would be used except when the gender reference could not be disguised. Second, the number of descriptors used in each of the nine categories would equal the mean number obtained for each gender or, if the mode were two or more units from the mean, an average of these measures. If the number of descriptors yielding gender differences within a category were less than the mean, words clustering with the significant descriptors or those having the highest frequency for the referent gender would be added. If the number of significant descriptors were greater than the mean, those having the lowest frequency would be removed.

Efforts to replicate the tone, style, and structure of actual FitRep narratives would include taking typical comments verbatim from the evaluations for the appropriate gender, paraphrasing them as necessary, and typing the narratives on an official form.

RESULTS

Reliability of Coders

The interrater reliabilities were very high. The unitizing reliability (difference between coders in recognizing a unit of material to be coded) was .001; and the content reliability (consistency between coders in assigning coding categories to the unit), .981. Because the two research assistants who developed the descriptor list also independently analyzed the content of the narratives, most differences over ambiguous cue words appear to have been resolved during the development phase.

Descriptors

Number

Table 6.2 presents the mean number of descriptors within each category included in narratives for women and men sample members and the results of the tests for gender differences. For the categories of manner of performance, personality traits, relations with others, self-expression, Navy variables, and leadership and management/administration, there was no significant difference in the mean number of descriptors applied to each gender. However, for the categories of combat performance, recommendations, and impact on Navy/command, men had significantly more descriptors than did women. The overall means for the two groups indicate that men's narratives contained more information than did the women's; the modes indicate that the most frequently occurring FitRep for women contained 15 descriptors, compared to 20 for men.

Table 6.2
Mean Number of Descriptors by Category
in Women's and Men's FitRep Narratives

| Information Category | Mean Number of Descriptors | | t-Test and Significance Level (df = 237) |
	Women	Men	
Manner of performance	4.66	4.77	−0.541
Personality traits	5.61	6.19	−1.554
Relations with others	1.85	2.13	−1.514
Self-expression	0.72	0.62	0.777
Combat performance	0.01	0.08	−2.409*
Recommendations	3.26	3.66	−2.496*
Navy variables	2.58	2.41	0.684
Leadership and management/administration	0.65	0.70	−0.515
Impact on Navy/command	1.64	2.13	−2.993**
Overall mean	20.97	22.70	11.107***
(Mode)	(15)	(20)	

*p < .05; **p < .01; ***p < .001.

Nature

Table 6.3 lists the descriptors used more frequently in the evaluations of one gender than the other. The majority of the differences favored men (negative z-ratio). In the Navy variables category, 6 of 13 descriptors showed gender differences; and in the impact on Navy/command category, 3 of the 12. Significantly more male officers than female officers were described as displaying Navy characteristics, having a supportive spouse, keeping physically fit, and having a positive impact on unit readiness, material facilities, and safety. Significantly more women than men were described as supporting equal opportunity principles, being well-groomed, and being a valuable asset to the command. For three categories—manner of performance, relations with others, and recommendations—only one descriptor showed significant gender differences. Finally, for the personality traits category, four descriptors showed significant differences.

Because recommendations for a specific assignment (605) are considered to be indicators of the overall potential of the officer being rated, this descriptor was analyzed further to determine the types of

Table 6.3

Descriptors in FitRep Narratives Yielding Significant Gender Differences

Category	Descriptor (Code Number)	Frequency		z-Ratio
		Women	Men	
Manner of performance	Competent/knowledgeable (102)	87	103	−2.696*
Personality traits	Logical/displays common sense (210)	15	28	−2.224*
	Dynamic (212)	8	21	−2.404*
	Mature/reliable (216)	17	37	−3.135**
	Aggressive (219)	18	39	−3.225**
Relations with others	Instructive (301)	22	50	−3.993***
Recommendations	Recommended for specific assignment (605)	47	79	−4.219***
Navy variables	Actively supports Navy Equal Opportunity Programs (710)	68	41	3.454***
	Well-groomed (704)	37	21	2.379*
	Valuable asset (706)	35	21	2.104*
	Possesses Navy characteristics (701)	17	30	−2.150*
	Keeps physically fit (703)	15	34	−3.084**
	Has a supportive spouse (707)	0	15	−4.029***
Impact on Navy command	On unit readiness (901)	8	27	−3.324***
	On material facilities (908)	9	23	−2.498*
	On safety (910)	6	20	−2.728**

*p < .05; **p < .01; ***P < .001.

recommendations made for each gender. As shown in Table 6.4, 37 of the men were recommended for command, probably the most important tour a naval officer can have at this stage of his or her career, compared to only 8 of the women. By contrast, almost equal numbers of both sexes were recommended for assignment to a service college. Such a recommendation accounted for half of all those made for women. Men's recommendations tended to be more oriented toward professional development as a naval officer.

Table 6.5 presents the results of a direct discriminant analysis conducted to investigate whether any of the personality descriptors differentiated between women and men. As shown, there were significant differences in four descriptors: aggressive, mature/stable, logical/displays common sense, and tactful. The discriminant function showed that the first three descriptors, which were identified by Broverman et al. (1972) as descriptive of the average man, were used to describe male officers. The last descriptor is a warmth-expressiveness characteristic, which Broverman et al. and this discriminant analysis found to be descriptive of women.

The cluster analyses, performed to identify the patterns of traits that clustered together in the narratives for women and men, are shown in Figure 6.1. The primary, stronger clusters are formed from traits with the highest correlations; and secondary clusters, from traits

Table 6.4

Recommendations for Specific Assignments Appearing in
Men's and Women's FitRep Narratives

	Frequency	
Recommended Assignment	Women	Men
Command	8	37
Service college	27	30
Specific assignment (recruiter, instructor, management)	10	18
Specific Navy course (LMET, SWOS, test pilot)	4	12
Department head	1	10
Executive officer	2	7
Tour in specialty/staff	2	3
Total number of recommendations	54	117

Note. Totals exceed the totals of women and men who received recommendations for a specific assignment (47 and 79, respectively) because persons were sometimes recommended for more than one assignment. This was true for 38 men, compared to only 7 women.

Table 6.5
Personality Descriptors in FitRep Narratives Discriminating
Between Male and Female Officers

Descriptor	Wilk's Lambda	Univariate F	p
Aggressive (219)	.95652	10.770	.0012
Mature/stable (216)	.95905	10.120	.0017
Logical/displays common sense (210)	.98064	6.249	.0131
Tactful (221)	.97431	4.678	.0316

df = 1237.

with decreasing correlations. For women the descriptors included in the primary cluster were initiative, sociable, tactful, logical, and intelligent; those included in the secondary cluster were energetic, assertive, and confident. For men the descriptors included in the primary cluster were aggressive, assertive, perceptive, initiative, and motivated; three descriptors—mature, sociable, and dependable—formed another, separate cluster. As anticipated, the strengths of association were low because the clustered traits were key words, representing many similar words (up to 19).

The differences in the female and male patterns are interesting. For example, for men confident was linked to tactful; for women, confident was linked to assertive. Also, the descriptors making up the primary cluster for the two genders are very different. Those in the women's primary cluster, with the exception of initiative, are thinking/feeling descriptors; those in the men's primary cluster, with the exception of perceptive, are competitive/active descriptors. The secondary clusters for both men and women consist of cross-sex descriptors.

Evaluation of Leadership and Management/Administrative

It was hypothesized that leadership behavior or potential would be discussed more often for the men than for the women and management/administrative abilities would be emphasized more for the women than for the men. Table 6.6 presents the frequencies of these descriptors and the results of the one-tailed test for gender differences.

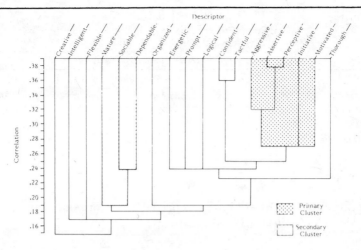

a. Clusters for male officers.

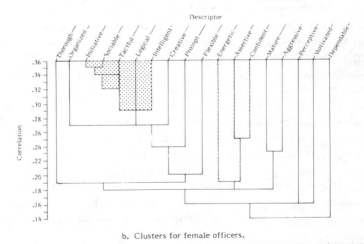

b. Clusters for female officers.

Figure 6.1. Results of single-linkage cluster analysis of personality traits in officer FitReps. The measure of similarity between traits (or groups of traits) is expressed as a correlation whose value is shown by the horizontal line at the bottom of the bar joining the traits. With male officers, for example, "assertive" and "perceptive" correlated .375. In the single-linkage solution, clusters are joined using the minimum distance rule. Thus "aggressive" is most similar to the first pairing and joins the initial cluster. The remaining traits belonging to that group are within the dotted area. A secondary cluster is formed of "mature," "sociable," and "dependable," intercorrelated traits that are distant from the primary cluster (i.e., not joined to it until late in the hierarchical procedure).

Table 6.6
Comparison of the Use of Leadership and
Management/Administration Descriptors in
Women's and Men's FitRep Narratives

| | Frequency | | |
Descriptor	Women	Men	z-ratio
Leadership	57	70	−1.756*
Management/administration	21	15	1.0589

*p < .05.

Although the results are in the expected direction, only the gender difference for leadership was significant.

Summary of Hypothesis Testing

Hypothesis 1 was supported by the data. These was no difference in the number of personality traits discussed in the narrative evaluations of the women and men, but the nature of these traits differed. Men, more so than women, were described as logical, dynamic, mature, and aggressive.

Hypothesis 2 was partly supported. The frequency with which descriptors of performance, relations with others, self-expression, and unique Navy variables were discussed in the FitRep narratives of women and men did not differ. The men's evaluations, however, provided more information about their anticipated performance in combat and the impact of their efforts on the Navy than did the women's. In addition, more specific recommendations and a greater number of recommendations were made in men's narratives than women's.

The nature of the descriptors appearing in some categories also differed. More male than female officers were described as being competent, effective in training others, marked by Navy characteristics, and physically fit, and as having a spouse who is an asset to their career. More women than men were described as supporting equal opportunity programs, appearing impeccable in their uniforms (well groomed), and being an asset to the command.

Hypothesis 3 was supported. Leadership skills were mentioned significantly more frequently in the men's narratives than in the women's; and management/administrative skills, more frequently (not significant) in the women's.

Impact on Selection Boards
of Differential Evaluations

Based on the results of the statistical analyses, two pseudo-FitRep narratives were written. Each included words found to describe the traits or performance of one sex more than the other,[4] as well as those used frequently in the evaluations of both sexes. The FitRep written for the male officer referred to LT Brown and that written for the female officer, to LT Smith. Also, instructions were prepared advising the pseudo-selection board members that both officers were highly qualified but only one could be recommended for promotion. The instructions and the two pseudo-FitRep narratives follow:

> You are a member of a Lieutenant Commander selection board. All of the candidates are so highly qualified that the enclosed two Fitness Reports are the only ones requiring a real decision. Your task is to recommend only one of these Lieutenants for promotion. The assumptions you will operate under are that both of these URL officers are in zone for the first time and a review of their previous FitReps has indicated that their assignment and performance in the Navy have been roughly parallel. The performance data and trends, rankings and recommendations on the front sides of their FitReps are identical, so the only information you have to work with is in the narrative section.

The male protocol stated:

> LT Brown has performed in a superlative manner as administrative officer of the submarine base. Mature, aggressive, and dynamic, Brown is an extremely forceful officer who carries out duties effectively.

> A true leader, Brown takes hold of a job and handles it with skill and technical know-how. Written work is always succinct, cogent, and presented as an excellent finished product. A self-starter, Brown has taken the initiative to upgrade the working environment of the division and has done a remarkable job. Also, under LT Brown's leadership and direction, the division has shown a notable improve-

ment in the condition of material facilities. LT Brown earns the respect of co-workers, subordinates, and higher-ups alike and is recognized as a true professional. Always sensitive to the needs of others, Brown has provided information necessary to teach others about opportunities available in the Navy and to direct them towards higher productivity. As a result of Brown's hard work and logical reasoning, the unit's standing and availability have improved considerably.

LT Brown is in top physical condition, maintains a rigorous exercise and fitness program, and is well-suited in character and temperament to naval life. This dedicated officer is highly recommended to a position of increased responsibility, accelerated promotion, and to post-graduate school.

The women's protocol read as follows:

LT Smith's performance has been superlative. As administrative officer of the submarine base, LT Smith has had to deal with complex civilian and military personnel situations and has done so with the utmost of tact and professionalism. Being responsible for a multitude of unrelated, yet important duties, this self-starter demonstrated the ability to establish sound priorities and to exercise the initiative it takes to get the job done in a timely manner. Smith has been instrumental in aiding the division's efforts and has earned praise from superiors for having had a positive impact on the unit's performance.

LT Smith is truly receptive to others, displaying a genuine concern for their welfare. Along these lines, the LT is a firm supporter of the Navy's EO program and its principles.

LT Smith is a bright, personable and outgoing officer whose impeccable appearance and articulate manner are a welcome addition to any group function and an asset to the Navy. LT Smith is an outstanding naval officer and is highly recommended for accelerated promotion to lieutenant commander.

The narratives were tested by asking 20 officers, lieutenant commander through captain, attending the Navy's prospective commanding officer/prospective executive officer (PCO/PXO) class in Coronado, California to review them and recommend one officer for promotion. Based on the comments of these officers, *all* of whom would have promoted LT Brown, three minor changes were made to the narratives. These changes were needed because some of the respondents had been influenced by nonstimulus words. Next, the amended pseudo-FitRep narratives were given to another PCO/PXO class and to students at the Naval Postgraduate School in Monterey, California. These experienced Navy officers would have overwhelmingly recommended LT Brown for selection to lieutenant commander, as shown in Table 6.7.

The comments written by these naval officers revealed the rationale for their choice. The more cogent ones are quoted here:

> The operative adjectives in LT Brown's comments convey power, ability, forcefulness, and leadership. In addition to getting the job done well, he leads, maintains an example (physical fitness).

> The words mature, aggressive, dynamic (Brown's) are more important in senior leadership positions than bright, personable, and outgoing (Smith's).

> It is likely that Brown is male and Smith is female—note the circled feminine qualities praised in Smith's report and masculine on Brown's even though use of gender pronouns has been scrupulously avoided. Brown's report also recommends PG school and positions of increased responsibility whereas Smith's does not. Smith is represented as a good "team player," while Brown is presented as a good "team leader."

The last comment was written by one of the six women officers in the sample, who had circled certain words in both FitRep narratives. She was obviously well in tune with the descriptors appearing in the narratives of Navy women.

Altogether, 48 of the 58 officers choosing LT Brown explained their choice, as did 5 of the 9 choosing LT Smith. The most frequently cited reasons for judging the male's narrative superior to the female's was the presence of phrases describing the impact of individual effort on the command and of specific recommendations. As one officer stated, "Brown's report describes an apparent push to get work done, while Smith's information does not suggest personal effort for improvement. Smith's success might be a halo of his/her troops doing a good job." Another officer keyed on the "flowery although nice descriptive comments for Smith. It seems the writer either unintentionally or purposely left out the specifics of the how done and results." Broverman et al. (1972) pointed out that such omissions could be indicative of stereotypical thought processes; that is, evaluators neglect to mention behavior subconsciously considered as

Table 6.7
Promotion Recommendations of Navy Officers
Based on Two Pseudo-Narratives

Sample	Officer Selected for Promotion	
	LT Brown (male)	LT Smith (female)
Postgraduate students (N = 53)	46	7
PCO/PXO class (N = 14)	12	2
Total	58	9

masculine. The few officers who chose LT Smith felt that her FitRep narrative was superior because it was more succinct, more general, and described a "manager par excellence."

This investigation demonstrated that there are differences in the words used to evaluate the performance of female and male line officers—differences not only in the content of the evaluations but also in the amount of information imparted. Interpreting these results without considering the organizational constraints on women's careers would lead to misconceptions. Despite the controls placed on the sample in terms of rank, years in service, and officer designator, the majority of female and male URL lieutenants in the Navy do not have similar jobs. Many of the men are aboard ships or in squadrons fulfilling true line functions, whereas most of the women are in offices performing support functions. Thus some of the differences in appraisals are understandable. Because women are not permitted to serve on combatant ships, there seems to be little reason to address their anticipated performance in combat. In addition, because few are assigned to operational commands, their efforts are less likely to have an impact on unit readiness, material facilities, and safety. Other differences, however, are hard to justify. Are women really less competent, logical, and mature, yet more valuable to their command than are men? Is their personal appearance in uniform more impeccable, although they exhibit less pride in the Navy than do men? Does their performance warrant few recommendations and only nebulous praise?

The goal of career Navy officers is to assume "command," but the commands that can be filled by women are severely limited. Commanding officers who write FitReps are usually from the same officer community as their subordinates. Their concept of command is a submarine, surface ship, air wing, or a shore station that is so related to these line commands that prior assignment in one is a prerequisite. Thus they write evaluations for male officers with these ultimate assignments in mind. In writing evaluations for female officers, Navy raters either assume that different qualities are needed in the commands women will hold or forget that women, too, have command as their goal.

The potential effect of gender-specific performance evaluations, however understandable, is disturbing. Male officers in the sample, of the appropriate rank to sit on selection boards, overwhelmingly judged the composite narrative of men to be more career enhancing than was that of women. When these officers were debriefed after participating in the forced-choice scenario, they acknowledged that the descriptors in the woman's narrative were consistent with those they had used in evaluating their female subordinates. Recognizing the strong influence that the absence of specific duty recommendations for the women had on their decision to select the man, they began to question what might have been said to increase her chances of selection. Very few knew what assignments would enhance a woman's career.

This research focused on women in a single organization, but there are implications for all women who compete with men in the professions, particularly those dominated by men. Schein (1978) identified several probable consequences of stereotyping on women's careers in management. First, if women are viewed as being more sensitive to the needs of others than are men, they are likely to be placed in staff versus line positions. As a result, they are less likely to acquire the skills and knowledge of the upwardly mobile. Second, if supervisors feel they lack the traits valued among managers and leaders (i.e., ambition, competitiveness, aggressiveness), women will be denied developmental tasks and their promotional potential will suffer. Third, women will be excluded from the organizational power network and thus be limited in their ability to function as effective managers.

In the military the behaviors and traits associated with the image of the leader/brave warrior define success. In other fields and professions the traits characterizing success may be different but, with few exceptions, are also masculine. Few women, even those of indisputable talent and competence, are viewed as measuring up to these images. Yet some will succeed and become leaders. Their success should affect how other aspiring women are perceived and evaluated, eventually blurring the image of the organizational "man."

NOTES

1. Officers who are not promoted (up) within a specified period are retired (out) from active duty.
2. This statute prevents women from serving aboard ships or aircraft having a combatant mission, over 90% of the operational billets in the Navy.
3. Words were considered in the context of the sentence in which they appeared. Moreover, care was taken to code separately similar phrases or words that have different meanings in the evaluations of naval officers. As an example, "should be promoted ahead of his contemporaries" is not the same as saying "should be promoted—now."
4. Reference to a spouse who is an asset was not included in the male protocol because of gender specificity.

REFERENCES

Bigoness, W. J. (1976). Effect of applicant's sex, race, and performance on employer performance ratings: Some additional findings. *Journal of Applied Psychology, 61*(1), 80-84.

Brinkerhoff, D. W., & Kanter, R. M. (1980, Spring). Appraising the performance of performance appraisal. *Sloan Management Review*, pp. 3-17.

Broverman, I. K., Vogel, S. R., Broverman, D. M., Clarkson, F. E., & Rosenkrantz, P. S. (1972). Sex-role stereotypes: A current appraisal. *Journal of Social Issues, 28*(2), 59-78.

Cardy, R. L., & Dobbins, G. H. (1984, August). *Affect and appraisal: The influence of liking on rating accuracy.* Paper presented at the 92nd Annual Convention of the American Psychological Association, Toronto, Canada.

Costrich, N., Feinstein, F., Kidder, L., Maracek, J., & Pascale, L. (1975). When stereotypes hurt: Three studies of penalties for sex role reversals. *Journal of Experimental Social Psychology, 11*, 520-530.

Deaux, K., & Taynor, J. (1973). Evaluation of male and female ability: Bias works two ways. *Psychological Reports, 32*, 261-262.

DeNisi, A. S., Cafferty, T. P., and Meglino, B. M. (1984). A cognitive view of the performance appraisal process: A model and research propositions. *Organizational Behavior and Human Performance, 33*, 360-396.

Frank, F., & Drucker, J. (1977). The influence of evaluatee's sex on evaluations of a response on a managerial selection instrument. *Sex Roles, 3*(1), 59-64.

Guetzkow, H. (1950). Unitizing and categorizing problems in coding qualitative data. *Journal of Clinical Psychology, 6*, 47-58.

Haering, G. (1980). Fitness report finesse. *U.S. Naval Institute Proceedings, 106*, 34-38.

Isaacs, M. B. (1981). Sex role stereotyping and the evaluation of the performance of women: Changing trends. *Psychology of Women Quarterly, 6*, 187-195.

Lenney, E., Mitchell, L., & Browning, C. (1983). The effect of clear evaluation criteria on sex bias in judgments of performance. *Psychology of Women Quarterly, 7*, 313-328.

Meyer, H. H., Kay, E., & French, J. R. P., Jr. (1965). Split roles in performance appraisal. *Harvard Business Review, 43*, 123-129.

Nieva, V. F., & Gutek, B. A. (1981). *Women and work: A psychological perspective.* New York: Praeger.

Paludi, M. A., & Strayer, L. A. (1985). What's in an author's name? Differential evaluations of performance as a function of author's name. *Sex Roles, 12*, 353-361.

Rosen, B., & Jerdee, T. H. (1973). The influence of sex-role stereotypes on evaluations of male and female supervisory behavior. *Journal of Applied Psychology, 57*(1), 44-48.

Schein, V. E. (1978). Sex role stereotyping, ability and performance: Prior research and new directions. *Personnel Psychology, 31*, 259-268.

Scott, W. A. (1955). Reliability of content analysis: The case of nominal scale coding. *Public Opinion Quarterly, 19*, 321-325.

Webster, M., & Driskell, J. E. (1978). Status generalization: A review and some new data. *American Sociological Review, 43*, 220-236.

Wiley, M. G., & Eskilson, A. (1982). Coping in the corporation: Sex role constraints. *Journal of Applied Social Psychology, 12*(1), 1-11.

Zedeck, S., & Cascio, W. F. (1984). Psychological issues in personnel decisions. *Annual Review of Psychology, 35*, 461-518.

7

Stepping onto the Academic Career Ladder
How Are Women Doing?

PHYLLIS BRONSTEIN, LEORA BLACK, JOYCE L. PFENNIG, and ADELE WHITE

Two studies conducted in two successive years each analyzed the credentials of applicants for a junior faculty position. They were used to compare male and female job candidates with respect to qualifications and the way they were depicted in their applications and letters of recommendation. The applicants were also followed to see what kind of job they eventually obtained. Men were more likely than women to apply for the faculty position and were more likely to have post-Ph.D. experience. Women were not evaluated less favorably than men in their letters of recommendation, which were generally free of sexism. Women were less likely than men to mention family status. Despite the positive presentation of female applicants, they were found in lower-status jobs in less prestigious institutions than their male counterparts when contacted a year and a half after the original study.

Changes in roles and expectations for women over the past 15 years have led to the increased enrollment of women in colleges and universities at all levels and a growing interest in professional careers.

Authors' Note: Portions of the research were presented at the meetings of the American Psychological Association, Washington, D.C., 1982 and Toronto, Canada, 1984. We wish to thank Chris Jeffrey for his help in processing the data.

110

More women than ever before are obtaining Ph.D.s and seeking entry-level appointments on academic faculties in areas that have traditionally been dominated by men. The field of psychology provides a good example of the current situation, in which there is increasing pressure to enable women to step onto the first rung of the academic career ladder. The most recently published American Psychological Association statistics on women and minorities in psychology (Russo, Olmedo, Stapp, & Fulcher, 1981) indicate that the percentage of academic positions that were held by women in the late 1970s was still relatively small, with women in graduate departments that offer the Ph.D making up only 21% of the faculty and 13% of the tenured faculty. In addition, in all academic settings women faculty were less likely to be tenured and more likely to have lower academic rank and part-time appointments. Moreover, although the percentage of unemployed Ph.D.s was small, women doctorate holders were more likely than their male counterparts to be unemployed and seeking employment.

On the other hand, the percentage of women doctorate recipients has increased markedly in recent years, from 27% in 1972 to 45.5% in 1982 (Committee on Women in Psychology, 1982-1983; Russo et al., 1981), and approximately half the students currently enrolled full-time in doctoral programs are women. Given this increasing pool of qualified women psychologists, can we assume, then, that departments are actively attempting to redress existing imbalances in their hiring of junior faculty? Are sufficient numbers of women now being hired to make a critical difference?

The answer is not so clear. Most affirmative action programs in academic institutions have as a stated goal that the percentage of women in each department must equal the percentage of women in the current availability pool in the respective discipline. That is, if 40% of qualified, available candidates for new positions are women, departments should strive to have faculties that are 40% female. Thus if the present imbalance were being widely redressed, one might expect to find an *over*representation of new female Ph.D.s in proportion to their numbers in entry-level academic positions, as psychology departments attempted to hire enough women to at least double the percentage of women on their faculties. Instead, the increase in the percentage of academic jobs going to new female Ph.D.s (from 31% to 41% between 1975 and 1978) seems merely to reflect the increase in the number of new female Ph.D.s during that period. In addition, the jobs they obtained during that period were still less likely to be tenure-track than those obtained by men (Stapp, Fulcher, Nelson, Pallak, & Wicherski, 1981).

Recent studies we conducted of the academic job application process in psychology, which we will describe here, suggest that things have not changed very much in the 1980s. A number of possible explanations for this slowness of change come to mind, which need to be explored:

(1) that there are disproportionately fewer Ph.D.-level women than men who are actually available for faculty positions, and that affirmative action efforts have been doing the best that can be expected with a limited resource;

(2) that women applicants tend to be less qualified than the men they are competing with and thus less often meet deparment hiring standards;

(3) that there are particular ways in which women applicants tend to be *perceived* that lead to the devaluation of both their competence (Lott, 1986; Nieva & Gutek, 1980; Thomas, this volume) and their desirability as professional colleagues.

Our data provide some useful clues about the part such factors may play in current academic hiring trends.

Briefly, we conducted two studies in two successive years, each one analyzing the credentials of applicants for a junior faculty position at an eastern state university. Because the first study had only a small number of female applicants and was based on a one-year rather than a tenure-track position (which might not have attracted a fully representative applicant pool), we have treated it more as a pilot and will focus mainly on the second. The findings for both were, in fact, very similar. We compared the contents of men's and women's *curriculum vitae* to see whether there were differences in their actual accomplishments, and content-analyzed and compared their letters of recommendation to see whether there were differences in how they were perceived and described by their recommenders. Our final step, after analyzing the *curriculum vitae* and letters, was to find out what became of the applicants—what jobs, if any, they ended up getting— and to compare this information with the credentials they had submitted, in relation to sex of applicant. We will present a few relevant findings in our discussion of item 1 above, followed by a more extensive description of the research in relation to items 2 and 3.

In considering the first of the possible explanations mentioned for current hiring practices, we noted that in both our samples there were substantially more male than female applicants. To see if this finding represented a broader trend, we obtained additional statistics during the two years of our research from the university of our samples and from another state university, both of which have doctoral programs in psychology. At the first, for five advertised junior-level positions in psychology (one one-year position and four tenure-track), an average of three times as many men as women applied. At the second for four advertised junior-level tenure-track positions in psychology, the average male-to-female applicant ratio was 4:1. So it may be that in spite of the fact that females now make up more than 45% of new psychology Ph.Ds, the overall number of females actually applying for academic jobs is small compared to the number of males. Why this may be the case is at present unclear. One explanation is that women, lacking the guidance and mentoring that their male counterparts have had, may be less oriented toward the traditional scholarly path and may be discovering that there are promising and lucrative opportunities for psychology Ph.D.s outside of academia. Of course, lack of mentoring and encouragement may also cause women to have lower aspirations for themselves and thus they may be hesitant to attempt that first step onto the academic ladder. A number of researchers have presented evidence that faculty tend to take women graduate students less seriously than they do men, and that they are less supportive of women graduate students' career plans (Brodsky, 1974; Freeman, 1972; Holmstrom & Holmstrom, 1974; Lewis, 1975; Sells, 1973). It may also be the case that as a result of encountering discrimination in academia during their graduate school years, some new female Ph.D.s are deciding to pursue less discouraging career paths.

Another possible reason for the low number of female applicants at the particular universities we sampled is that women are more likely than men to put family obligations ahead of their own career aspirations; thus they may be less willing or able to relocate, tending to seek jobs in large urban centers where their husbands can also find employment (Brodsky, 1974; Centra, 1974; Leviton & Whitely, 1981; Maxwell, Rosenfeld, & Spilerman, 1979; Solomon, 1976). With this hypothesis in mind we analyzed the mention of family status on applicants' *curriculum vitae* to see whether female applicants for a position at a *nonurban* university were more likely than male applicants to be single. If the women in our second study felt encumbered by family responsibility, they weren't telling anyone. Of the men, 51% listed their marital status on their *curriculum vitae*, but only 17% of the women did—and of those who mentioned it, 73% of the men indicated that they were married and 27% that they were single, whereas *all* of the women who listed it said that they were single. In addition, one-quarter of the male applicants in both studies reported the number of children they had, whereas not one female applicant reported having any. These data lead us to two possible conclusions: (1) Women with husbands or families tend not to apply for jobs away from urban centers, and all the women in our second sample were single and thus more mobile, (2) Women with husbands or families are applying for such jobs but have decided that reporting their family status is irrelevant or perhaps unwise. There is evidence to support the second conclusion. The women in our sample said nothing about having a family—but letters of recommendation for 25 of them mentioned husband or children.

Although lack of mentoring and family concerns may be contributing factors, there is another reason why the number of female applicants seems to be relatively low. Currently there are increasing numbers of "recycled" men on the job market—men who had found academic jobs several years earlier (at a time when there were substantially fewer female Ph.D.s) but who had only temporary appointments or were later denied reappointment or tenure, and who are now seeking another entry-level position. Our data support this. Male applicants, on the average, had earned their degrees one and a half years earlier than female applicants, and 47% of the males (versus 25% of the females) had earned them three or more years prior to applying for the position.

We next considered the other two explanations suggested for current hiring trends—that women tend to be less qualified than the men with whom they are competing or that they tend to be *perceived* as less qualified and less desirable as professional colleagues. For the first, our research provides new data, in that previously published studies of women's and men's qualifications have looked at the publication and citation rates of established professionals and not of "newly minted" psychology Ph.D.s. Several of these studies have found that women publish less and are cited less often then men (Helmreich, Spence, Beane, Lucher, & Matthews, 1980; Over, 1982) but that there is no difference between men and women in the number of citations per published paper (Over, 1982). However, Guyer and Fidell's (1973) findings suggest that this holds true only at the associate and full professor levels, and Goldstein (1979) found no difference between women's and men's publishing rates four years after receiving the Ph.D.

For the second explanation, although we had no data on how applicants were perceived by various hiring deparments, we did have their letters of recommendation—and we reasoned that those letters, in presenting referees' perceptions and evaluations of applicants' competence, might have been susceptible to the kinds of biases that have been noted in previous research on the evaluation of women (Fidell, 1970; Goldberg, 1968; Levin & Duchan, 1971; Lott, 1986; Pheterson, Kiesler & Goldberg, 1971). There is, in addition, evidence to suggest that different kinds of recommendations may be written for women than for men. Studies of letters written for various academic departments have shown lower levels of praise for women, less recognition for women's intellectual ability and achievements, less favorable perception of women in a present or future professional role, greater inclusion of irrelevant facts about women's lives (such as family status or age), and sexist references to women's appearance and personality traits (Guillemin, Holmstrom, & Garvin, 1979; Hoffman, 1972; Lewis, 1975; Lunneborg & Lillie, 1973)—although Farley (1978), analyzing a large sample of letters for women's studies positions in the 1970s, found that the mention of women's appearance and marital status had diminished greatly by 1978. Given the predominant findings from these studies, it seemed likely that we might find differences detrimental to women applicants in the letters of the present studies and in the areas of intellectual ability and achievement, perceptions of professional role and future success, inclusion of facts irrelevant to the job requirements, and sexist references to appearance and personality. Moreover, we might expect these differences to show up further if we compared referees' evaluations of women and men with the applicants' actual qualifications, detailed in their *curriculum vitae.*

A REPORT OF THE RESEARCH

In our detailing of the research project, we will present only those findings which were relevant to points raised earlier or which were part of a general trend in both studies. Any additional findings (of which there were very few) have been regarded as idiosyncratic to the particular sample and have been omitted. In addition, because we regard our first study as more of a pilot, we will present it in abbreviated form.

Study 1

Method

Our sample consisted of the credentials that were submitted in response to an ad in the employment section of the *APA Monitor* for a one-year assistant professorship in clinical psychology at an eastern state university with a clinical doctoral program. Specifically, we examined the *curriculum vitae* of the 76 applicants (60 males and 16 females), plus the 289 letters of recommendation that accompanied them, from 244 male referees, 44 female referees, and one whose sex was not determinable. In analyzing the *curriculum vitae*, we recorded all personal information provided by applicants (such as sex, age, and family status), relevant facts about their degree (including year, area, prestige of institution, and whether the program was APA approved), and multiple measures of their research productivity, including primary or secondary authorship, and numbers and kinds of publications, presentations, and grants. Because employment experience, internships, assistantships, and the like were too difficult to evaluate from the information given, we did not include them. In analyzing the letters we noted and then removed all information identifying persons or institutions, in order both to protect the privacy of the applicants and their recommenders and to allow for blind coding of the contents. We then had them coded twice. The first time two research assistants recorded on 23 category cards all mentions of main areas of skill (such as teaching, research, or clinical practice), all phrases praising or criticizing the applicant, and all mentions of facts irrelevant to the job requirements (such as appearance, family status, or athletic ability). At the same time, coders removed all references to gender. Agreement between coders for five letters coded independently averaged 75%, with disagreement occurring mainly when one coder broke a phrase down more finely and recorded it in two categories rather than in one. A more detailed system with 41 categories was then developed from this preliminary coding, consisting of areas of competency and praise (such as research productivity, teaching skill, motivation, and self-presentation as a professional), positive qualifiers and superlatives (e.g., "solid," "outstanding"), criticisms or reservations, and irrelevant facts. Three additional coders recoded the phrases from the category cards, with agreement between pairs of coders averaging 78%. Total frequencies within each category were then calculated for each letter.

Results

Differences revealed in the *curriculum vitae* of female and male applicants and differences in the characteristics of female and male referees were essentially the same for both studies, and therefore will be discussed only in relation to the second study. Two-way analyses of variance performed on the skill and praise categories of the letters by sex of referee and sex of applicant showed two significant and two near-significant main effects for sex of applicant. Female applicants were cited significantly more often for their intelligence ($F(1,284) = 13.58, p > .001$) and their self-presentation as a professional ($F(1,284) = 4.23, p < .05$), were more often described in terms of their professional role ($F(1,284) = 3.14, p < .08$), and were more often cited for their competence, in particular by male referees ($F(1,284) = 3.66, p < .06$). In addition, there was one significant interaction; female applicants were more often cited by female referees for their motivation/commitment ($F(1,284) = 4.22, p < .05$). Thus all trends and significant differences favored *female* applicants.

We found that with the exception of references to age (e.g., "promising young psychologist"), for which there were no sex differences, very few instances of inclusion of irrelevant material occurred. Our expectation for traditional perceptions of men and women applicants were only minimally met; six male referees mentioned the sports involvement of male applicants and three male referees mentioned the appearance of female candidates. On the other hand, family status was mentioned 22 times—but in each case by a male referee about a *male* applicant, with no relationship between a referee's mention of it and the applicant's own mention of it in the *curriculum vitae*.

For the next phase of the analysis, we averaged the frequency scores for each category across all of an applicant's letters to compensate for differences among applicants in the number of letters submitted (there were no sex differences in number of letters per applicant). These mean frequencies were used in all subsequent analyses. We then correlated the various measures of research productivity from the *curriculum vitae* with the relevant skill and praise categories of the letters, to see whether the letters in fact accurately portrayed the accomplishments of the applicants as they had been listed in the *curriculum vitae*. We found that referees' mention of applicants' research productivity did correlate highly with measures of actual research productivity (e.g., with total number of publications, $r(74) = .50$, $p < .001$; with number of primary authored articles, $r(74) = .46$, $p < .001$; and with total number of conference presentations, $r(74) = .40$, $p < .001$). Actual research productivity also correlated highly with mention of the applicant as a professional in the field and with a description of the applicant as being respected. In addition, it correlated moderately (though still significantly) with such relevant letter categories as analytic ability, having extensive knowledge or background in an area, the total number of superlative qualifiers (e.g., "excellent," "outstanding," "the best") describing the applicant, and the total amount of praise given in all categories. Thus it appeared that referees had given realistic evaluations of applicants when describing qualities related to research productivity, and those findings held up when the same correlations were done separately for female and male applicants.

Finally, we performed t-tests on the various praise categories to see whether there were differences in the mean frequency scores in how males and females were described. Males were cited significantly more often for research productivity ($t(74) = 2.09$, $p < .05$), which is consonant with the fact that the *curriculum vitae* of male applicants showed significantly higher research productivity, a finding that will be discussed in the following section. On the other hand, there were two significant differences (as well as several nonsignificant trends) in which female applicants were higher. As was found in the earlier analysis of the nonaveraged letter data, women were more often cited for their positive self-presentation as a professional, with $t(74) = 2.20$, $p < .05$, and for their intelligence, with $t(74) = 2.66$, $p = .01$. Overall there were very few differences, but again, what differences there were generally favored females.

Study 2

The second study—of applications for an advertised tenure-track assistant professorship in social psychology at the same university—was carried out the following year.

Method

Our sample consisted of the *curriculum vitae* of the 97 candidates who applied for the position (66 males and 31 females), plus the 329 letters that accompanied them, from 277 male and 51 female referees, and one letter from a group of graduate students. The *curriculum vitae* were coded in the same manner as the first study. In analyzing the letters, basic information identifying persons, gender, institutions, and professional and institutional status were first noted, and then all names, titles, institutional references, and indications of gender were removed to protect the privacy of the applicants and their recommenders and to allow for blind coding of the data. There were 32 coding categories; 9 categories from the initial 41 of the first study were either eliminated or combined with others because of low frequency of occurrence. Coding of the letters was done by a coder from the first study and by the second author (LB). The latter's coding reliability was established by LB and the senior author independently coding three letters; agreement between them on the 238 phrases that they both coded was 86%, decreasing to 60% when phrases coded by one coder but not the other were counted as disagreements. Then, as in the first study, total frequencies within each category were calculated for each letter, and the *curriculum vitae* and letter data were analyzed for sex differences.

Results

For the *curriculum vitae*, many findings replicated those of the first study. Using a combined list of the rankings done by Roose and Andersen (1970), Cox and Catt (1977), and Endler, Rushton, and Roediger (1978), we compared the quality ratings of the doctoral programs of female and male applicants and found no significant difference—although in both studies a somewhat higher percentage of women came from leading programs. Looking next at research productivity, we found that men were higher than women on 17 of 22 measures of publication and presentation and significantly so on 5, including total number of publications, total first author publications, first author publications in both highly cited journals (listed in White & White, 1977; Rushton & Roediger, 1978; Garfield 1979) and less cited journals, and secondary author conference presentations. However, in both studies when we regressed the various measures of publication and presentation on sex of applicant, controlling for years since receiving the doctorate, all relationship between sex and publication/presentation quantity disappeared. It appears that the sex difference was entirely accounted for by the fact that men had been in the world of professional psychology longer ($\overline{X} = 1.5$ years) and had thus had more time to conduct, present, and publish research. There was no difference in the *rate* of publication for female and male applicants.

For the letters, referee characteristics were essentially the same as in the first study. Not surprisingly, given the overall scarcity and low status of women in graduate departments, there were 5.5 times as many male as female referees, and female referees had significantly lower academic status ($F(1,323) = 16.96$, $p < .001$). However, there were no sex differences in institutional status.

Among referees there was a significant tendency to support same-sex applicants, especially for female referees. Although only one-third of the applicants were female, female referees wrote 51% of their letters for female applicants, whereas male referees wrote 28% for females and 72% for males ($\chi^2(2) = 11.22$, $p < .01$). Looking separately at male and female referees' perceptions and evaluations of male and female applicants, we found no interpretable patterns of significant findings. However, we did find a general trend in numerous categories for the highest amount of praise to have been given by female referees for female applicants and the lowest amount of praise to have been given by female referees for male applicants. When we obtained average category frequency scores across letters for each candidate and then performed t-tests, we found only one significant sex difference: There were significantly more reservations and criticisms expressed about male than about female applicants ($t(95) = 2.36$, $p < .05$). Again, measures of actual research productivity from the *curriculum vitae* correlated significantly with relevant skill and praise categories of the letters (though to a lesser degree than in the first study), indicating that referees to some extent had accurately portrayed applicants' accomplishments.

Looking at the mention of facts irrelevant to the job requirements, we found again that with the exception of references to age, it very seldom occurred. Moreover, when it did occur, it was much more likely to be about a man than about a woman—though usually in a complimentary way ("He's a first-rate folk musician," or "He plays a mean game of chess"). Appearance was mentioned 12 times—three times as often for men as for women! The few references there were to women's appearance were inoffensive ("She's an able, attractive, warm, supportive person"). Family mention, however, was another matter; although it occurred infrequently, it was the only variable in the study for which the raw frequencies were higher for women than for men, even though there were only half as many women as men in the sample. Reference to family or marital status was made 17 times for men and 22 times for women ($F(1,324) = 3.51$, $p = .06$).

DISCUSSION

Our research provides data that begin to answer two important questions: Are women applicants for junior faculty positions in psychology as qualified as the men they are competing with, and are they *perceived* as equally competent and desirable as professional colleagues? For the samples studied here, the answer to the first question is clearly yes. Female applicants came from equally (or more highly) ranked doctoral programs, with degrees in the areas in which the jobs were offered—and in the case of the clinical position equally as often they had received degrees from APA-approved clinical programs. They published and presented their research at the same rate as male applicants, and in letters of recommendation they tended to be praised more and criticized less than their male counterparts.

For the second question, in terms of how women were perceived and evaluated by the teachers, supervisors, and mentors who wrote their letters of recommendation, we considered the data in relation to our initial hypotheses of sex differences detrimental to women applicants. Our findings were almost all directly counter to our expectations.

(1) Level of praise. Women tended to receive more praise than men, in a number of different areas, from both female and male referees in the first study and from female referees in the second.

(2) Intellectual ability and achievement. In both studies women were cited more often than men for their intelligence—significantly so in the first study. Regarding achievement, there were no differences between male and female applicants for the mention of skill areas (e.g., teaching, research, administration), but men were cited more often for research productivity and significantly so in the first study. This, however, was an accurate reflection of men's higher level of publication and presentation.

(3) Present and future professional role. For the three revelant variables (positive self-presentation as a professional, being referred to in a professional role, and prediction of future success), the differences in both studies, whether slight or substantial, all favored women.

(4) Irrelevant information. There were no consistent tendencies across studies for the inclusion of irrelevant information about women—in fact, more irrelevant information was included about men, though usually in a complimentary way. Family mention, however, though not consistently occurring more frequently for women applicants, took on a very different cast, depending on whether a man or a woman was being described. For men having a family was presented as an asset:

> His lovely wife and two children are an additional bonus for a department that has any kind of social life.

> He has the good fortune to be married to _____, also an excellent psychologist, and a fine contributor to the research environment.

For a woman, however, it was presented as a burden:

> As one might expect from a woman who has returned to graduate school after taking several years off to raise young children . . .

> I have to chuckle when I hear some of our other graduate students complain about being overburdened, when I think of how much she gets done at the same time, as she is a mother to two children and a wife to an administrator.

> At the same time she was accomplishing all this, she has also been an excellent parent to her two children, caring for them, being there whenever she was needed, taking an active interest in their schooling, as well as being an enthusiastic supporter of their sports and recreational activities.

Although these examples may represent reality, in terms of women's greater responsibility for family work (Schwartz & Blumstein, 1983), as well as their ability to handle both family and career, we can only wonder at the reactions of search committee members attempting to consider who would be more willing to relocate and who would make the most promising and productive junior faculty member.

(5) Sexist references to appearance and personality traits. The few references to women's appearance that were present were found inoffensive, nondetrimental, and not substantially different from references made to men's appearance (which occurred more frequently). Any negative comments about personality were scored as criticism—and that category was higher for male applicants in both studies.

Overall, then, referees were supportive and nonsexist in their evaluations of female applicants. In addition, though there was evidence of "old boys'" networks in operation, in that male referees wrote the major proportion of their letters for male applicants, "old girls'" networks seemed to be developing as well, as witnessed by the greater proportion of letters women wrote for women in the second study and the overall higher level of praise and support in those letters. Female applicants and referees also seemed to be aware of the potentially detrimental effects of detailing women's domestic commitments, so that not one female applicant in the second study acknowledged having husband or children, and the referees who mentioned them were almost always male. There may be some cause for concern about the way women's family responsibilities were portrayed, although it seems likely that those referees were in fact praising the applicants for their competence and may have been unaware of the unintended effects their comments might have.

FOLLOW-UP

A year and a half after each position was advertised, we sent a follow-up letter with a return postcard to everyone who had applied, asking about their current career status. Since only a third of the applicants in the first study returned the cards, we did not analyze those data. However, 80% of the applicants in the second study returned the cards, due probably to the greater persistence on our part in locating them and to a more effective cover letter. They reported when they had finished their degree, the details of the position they had eventually obtained for 1982-1983, and (because they received our request in the summer of 1983), their plans for the coming 1983-1984 academic year. Their responses provided some interesting and provocative information. Although the sex differences were not statistically significant, they revealed a consistent overall pattern, which may be indicative of current academic hiring trends.

(1) By September 1983, 96% of the men and 86% of the women had received their Ph.D. A total of 95% of both men and women had held full-time positions for 1982-1983, decreasing to 89% for 1983-1984, and for both years approximately 90% had psychology-related jobs. A total of 74% of the men and 68% of the women had academic teaching jobs for 1982-1983, which had evened out to about 70% each for 1983-1984. Thus the actual *numerical* sex ratio for hiring by academic departments for this particular sample was approximately 2:1 male. There was no overrepresentation of females in proportion to their numbers in the hiring of this sample for entry-level positions.

(2) Males had higher salaries, with the discrepancy approaching statistical significance. However, when earnings were regressed on sex of applicant, controlling for years since receiving the doctorate, all relationship between earnings and sex of applicant disappeared. Earnings were related strictly to time since receiving the doctorate and not to sex per se.

(3) For both years an average of 63% of the male applicants but only 42% of the female applicants had academic positions at the assistant professor level or higher, which is a greater discrepancy than can be explained by the 10% fewer women having finished their degree by that time.

(4) Averaged over the two years, 80% of the men but only 69% of the women had positions in universities, medical schools, or prestigious four-year colleges. Fully 28% of the women but only 11% of the men had positions at low-prestige four-year or two-year colleges.

(5) Over the two years an average of 81% of earlier Ph.D. recipients (defined as those who received their Ph.D. before 1980) had academic teaching jobs, as compared to 64% of later recipients. Further, 77% of earlier recipients had academic jobs at the assistant professor level or higher, as compared to only 47% of later recipients. Thus earlier, "recycled" Ph.D. recipients did substantially better on the job market than later recipients—and 79% of that earlier recipient group were men.

Thus although the women in our sample were at least as well qualified as the men, they tended to obtain jobs with lower status and at lower-prestige institutions. These findings suggest that inequities do exist at the entry level for women seeking academic jobs. Equally disturbing, however, are the implications for career advancement. Raelin (1982), in a study of early career progress of women and men, found that the prestige of the first job is crucial to early career success for women and is more important for women than for men. Peters and Ceci (1982) found that prestige of institution is apparently an important factor in acceptance for articles submitted to psychology journals that use non-blind review. Thus entry-level inequities may have long-term deleterious effects on women's career development.

One explanation for the inequities at the entry level might be that departments prefer to hire faculty with more publications and experience, and because there are more "recycled" men than women on the job market, men are more frequently hired and at a higher level and at more prestigious places. To test this within our sample, we compared the job outcomes of our "recycled" earlier recipients. We found that 78% of the men but only 67% of the women had academic jobs at the assistant professor level or higher, and 84% of the men as opposed to 67% of the women had jobs in higher-prestige institutions. On the other hand, 33% of the women but only 12% of the men had jobs in lower-prestige institutions. Thus for more experienced applicants, the pattern was the same: Men did better than women. What this means for this particular sample in terms of numbers rather than percentages, given that it included more than twice as many males as females, is that over both years twice as many men as women were hired for academic jobs, more than three times as many men as women obtained jobs at the assistant professor level or higher, and more than twice as many men as women got jobs at higher-prestige institutions whereas more women than men got jobs at lower-prestige institutions. Clearly this pattern of hiring suggests that present affirmative action efforts may not be sufficient to correct the existing 5:1 gender imbalance within graduate departments of psychology.

We believe the data from our two studies shed light on what is currently happening for women attempting to step onto the first rung of the academic career ladder. What they do not shed light on is *"why?"* Perhaps because there is a surfeit of qualified (and overqualified) men seeking jobs at the junior faculty level, departments are ignoring affirmative action pressures in the interest of hiring applicants who have had time to develop proven track records (i.e., men). Or perhaps the hiring process involves more subtle procedures and decisions, in which preconceptions and misperceptions of women come into play, so that departments purportedly trying to hire qualified women keep coming up empty-handed. Qualified women are clearly out there in increasing numbers seeking academic jobs. Our research, coupled with research on the hiring process itself and, more generally, the evaluation process (see Thomas, this volume; Nieva & Gutek, 1980), is crucial to understanding the continuing underrepresentation of women in the faculty ranks of graduate departments of psychology.

REFERENCES

Brodsky, A. (1974). Women as graduate students. *American Psychologist, 29*, 523-529.

Centra, J. A. (1974). *Women, men, and the doctorate.* Morristown, NJ: Educational Testing Service.

Committee on Women in Psychology. (1982-1983). *Women in the American Psychological Association.* Annual Report. Washington, DC: American Psychological Association.

Cox, W. M., & Catt, V. (1977). Productivity ratings of graduate programs in psychology based on publication in the journals of the American Psychological Association. *American Psychologist, 32,* 793-812.

Endler, N. S., Rushton, J. P., & Roediger, H. L. (1978). Productivity and scholarly impact (citations) of British, Canadian, and U.S. departments of psychology (1975). *American Psychologist, 33,* 1064-1082.

Farley, J. (1978). Academic recommendations: Males and females as judges and judged. *AAUP Bulletin, 64,* 82-85.

Fidell, L. S. (1970). Empirical verification of sex discrimination in hiring practices in psychology. *American Psychologist, 25,* 1094-1098.

Freeman, J. (1972). *How to discriminate against women without really trying.* Unpublished manuscript, Department of Political Science, University of Chicago.

Garfield, E. (1979). *Citation indexing: Its theory and application in science, technology and humanities.* New York: John Wiley.

Goldberg, P. (1968, April). Are women prejudiced against women? *Transaction,* pp. 28-30.

Goldstein, E. (1979). Effect of same-sex and cross-sex models on the subsequent academic productivity of scholars. *American Psychologist, 34,* 407-410.

Guillemin, J., Holmstrom, L. L., & Garvin, M. (1979, February). Judging competence: Letters of recommendation for men and women faculties. *School Review,* pp. 157-170.

Guyer, L., & Fidell, L. (1973). Publications of men and women psychologists: Do women publish less? *American Psychologist, 28*(2), 157-160.

Helmreich, R. L., Spence, J. T., Beane, W. E., Lucher, G. W., & Matthews, K. A. (1980). Making it in academic psychology: Demographic and personality correlates of attainment. *Journal of Personality and Social Psychology, 39,* 896-908.

Hoffman, N. J. (1972). Sexism in letters of recommendation: A case for consciousness raising. *Modern Language Association Newsletter,* Winter, *4,* 4-5.

Holmstrom, E. T., & Holmstrom, R. (1974). The plight of the woman doctoral student. *American Educational Research Journal, 11,* 1-17.

Levin, A. Y., & Duchan, L. (1971, September 3). Women in academia. *Science, 173,* 892-895.

Leviton, L. C., & Whitely, S. E. (1981). Job-seeking patterns of female and male Ph.D. recipients. *Psychology of Women Quarterly, 5,* 690-701.

Lewis, L. S. (1975). *Scaling the ivory tower: Merit and its limits in academic careers.* Baltimore: Johns Hopkins University Press.

Lott, B. (1986). The devaluation of women's competence. *Journal of Social Issues, 41*(4), 43-60.

Lunneborg, P. W., & Lillie, C. (1973). Sexism in graduate admissions: The letter of recommendation. *American Psychologist, 28*(2), 187-189.

Maxwell, G., Rosenfeld, R., & Spilerman, S. (1979, September 21). Geographic constraints on women's careers in academia. *Science, 205,* 1225-1231.

Nieva, V. F., & Gutek, B. A. (1980). Sex effects in evaluation. *Academy of Management Review, 5,* 267-276.

Over, R. (1982). Research productivity and impact of male and female psychologists. *American Psychologist, 37*(1), 24-31.

Peters, D., & Ceci, S. J. (1982). Peer review practices of psychological journals: The fate of published articles, submitted again. *Behavioral and Brain Sciences, 5,* 187-196.

Pheterson, G., Kiesler, S. B., & Goldberg, P. A. (1971). Evaluation of the performance of women as a function of their sex, achievement, and personal history. *Journal of Personality and Social Psychology, 19*(1), 114-118.

Raelin, J. A. (1982). A comparative analysis of female-male early youth careers. *Industrial Relations, 21*, 231-247.

Roose, K. D., & Andersen, C. J. (1970). *A rating of graduate programs.* Washington, DC: American Council on Education.

Rushton, J. P., & Roediger, H. L. (1978). An evaluation of 80 psychology journals based on the *Science Citation Index. American Psychologist, 33*, 520-523.

Russo, N. F., Olmedo, E. L., Stapp, J., & Fulcher, R. (1981). Women and minorities in psychology. *American Psychologist, 36*, 1315-1363.

Schwartz, P., & Blumstein, P. (1983). *American couples: Money, work and sex.* New York: William Morrow.

Sells, L. (1973). *Sex differences in graduate school survival.* Paper presented at the annual meeting of the American Sociological Association, New York.

Solomon, L. C. (1976). *Male and female graduate students: The question of equal opportunity.* New York: Praeger.

Stapp, J., Fulcher, R., Nelson, S. D., Pallak, M. S., & Wicherski, M. (1981). The employment of recent doctorate recipients in psychology: 1975 through 1978. *American Psychologist, 36*, 1211-1254.

White, M. J., & White, K. G. (1977). Citation analysis of psychology journals. *American Psychologist, 32*, 301-305.

8

A Comparison of the Career Paths Used by Successful Women and Men

LAURIE LARWOOD and URS E. GATTIKER

A study of the career development of 215 successful personnel in seventeen major firms examined the paths respondents had taken and the levels of hierarchical success attained. The results show long-term movement toward professional and higher positions within the department and indicate the manner in which professional status, line positions, and higher-level positions are associated with hierarchical success. Older and younger women have substantially the same levels of success and have attained similar situations at the same time, whereas younger men appear to lag behind older men. These and other findings are interpreted as supportive of a "dual development" model of careers suggesting that women's careers cannot be entirely understood by reference to the patterns of men's careers. The results may be of practical importance to career planners and of theoretical significance in the areas of career development and sex roles.

In discussing career development organizational theorists have largely taken either of two positions. One position, which might be labeled the "classic model," is quite simply that career patterns are typified by the careers traditionally expected of successful males. Such a position ignores the influence of the unique social and family situations of women and also attaches little significance to demands

Authors' Note: Portions of this chapter were presented at the 1984 annual meetings of the Academy of Management, Boston, and American Psychological Association, Toronto.

on men external to the work environment. For example, in their survey of thinking and practice, Gutteridge and Otte (1983, p. 6) define organizational career development quite simply as the "outcomes of the interaction between individual career planning and institutional career management processes," with no mention of gender, family, or external demands. Similar thinking has been expressed by others (e.g., Schein, 1971), sometimes in an effort to distinguish between organizationally relevant issues and influences that initially appear relevant only on the personal or social levels (London & Stumpf, 1982, pp. 4-5).

A more circumspect alternative to the model above is a "neoclassic model" of organizational development in which theorists agree that competing family demands and individual preferences may interact with organizational needs to affect careers (see Hall, 1976). In some cases those proposing these models have suggested explicitly that because of the inclusions, the models apply as well to women as to men; nonetheless, women's careers are generally discussed only by limited exception to rules intended to apply to men's organizational career development (Hall, 1976, pp. 33-36; Schein, 1978, pp. 49-61).

Recently some investigators have begun questioning whether the neoclassic model is itself sufficiently enlightened. Osipow (1983, p. 271) concluded a review of the literature concerning women's career interests and preparation by stating that research exists both to the effect that women are similar to men in their interests (thus that existing concepts are sufficient) and that they are dissimilar (and existing concepts are insufficient). Nonetheless, Osipow agrees with some other observers that even women who are otherwise identical to men face fundamentally different situations in developing careers than do men (Brooks, 1984; Souerwine, 1978, p. 240; Stewart & Gudykunst, 1982). That is, problems such as sex discrimination and opportunities such as emphasis on equal employment may have substantially altered women's patterns of career development from those of men.

The present study applies this third "dual development" model in examining the development of men's and women's careers in organizations over an extended period of time. Although loosely defined by the research cited earlier, the model suggests that any understanding of the careers of men and women requires consideration not only of family and competing demands external to the work environment but of phenomena that may distinguish between men and women. Such a model would seem necessary to understand careers in view of events such as military draft and improved birth control techniques which have a more immediate impact on the lives of one sex than on the other. In this study we propose that the careers of women are in fact substantially different from those of men—that the pattern of women's careers is in part tied to women's less advantageous position in the job market, as discussed below. Although we gathered information concerning other career aspects, this article is restricted to the interrelationships, over time, of antecedent job situation and later hierarchical success.

Only demonstrably "successful" individuals were examined, in agreement with Osipow's (1983, p. 271) suggestion that prior research may have been inconclusive because it often mixed respondents at varying levels of success. Although this study was conducted at a single point in time, the data are retrospective, encompassing the entire span of participants' careers. With the most notable recent exceptions being Raelin's (1982) examination of early careers, Rosenbaum's (1984, 1985) longitudinal analysis in a single firm, and Spenner, Otto, and Call's (1982) analysis of synthetic census cohort careers, few studies have attempted to take more than a single period "snapshot" of careers. As a result, they can assess success and antecedent preparation but cannot readily determine the manner in which preparation and intervening decisions led to the present situation. Empirical evidence to that effect would seem to be necessary in determining how the level of success was in fact achieved, in creating and testing alternative models of organizational career development, and in advising women and men on how they might improve their situations (Brooks, 1984).

RESEARCH FOCUS

The next sections are directed at three different kinds of predictions. Following the classic model, we expected to find that job situations are systematically linked across time and lead to hierarchical success. Consistent with the neoclassic model of career development, however, the subsequent section suggests that women would be found to differ from men by being "behind" them in development—possibly as the result of discrimination. A third section applies the dual development model in predicting that women's career development does not merely follow that of men but may actually proceed in a different manner. A final section summarizes the most important predictions.

Job Situation

Both individual and organizational research indicate that one of the best predictors of a situation at any point in time is having been in that same situation in the recent past (see Berlew & Hall, 1976). One explanation for this stability lies in people's efforts to maintain consistent views of themselves and to resist entering situations that might require self-concept change (Bem, 1972; Tedeschi, Schlenker, & Bonoma, 1971). Possible change (self-perception) may be avoided if one's behavior agrees with preexisting views of self—which it generally does, at least among those with high self-esteem (Biddle, 1979, p. 325; Korman, 1976; Lopez, 1982). For example, students have been shown to select college majors having stereotypes aligned with their self-concepts and to change majors toward more congruence with their self-concepts (Backman & Secord, 1968). Organizations have greater turnover among those with self-concepts incongruent to their careers (Weiner & Vaitenas, 1977). Thus it seems likely that people who are successful would have moved in the past toward situations associated with and leading to success.

In particular, it was anticipated that higher department levels, more professionalism, and greater centrality would lead to hierarchical organizational success. If that were true, we also anticipated that the sample of successful individuals would show successive increases in measures of these variables as their careers progressed. In fact, research does indicate that those who seem successful early are expected to continue to succeed and are given the opportunity to do so (Berlew & Hall, 1976; Eden & Ravid, 1982)—even when initial success is apparently a matter of random assignment. Similarly, Rosenbaum (1984) found that those who were promoted early were more likely to be promoted again in later periods than those promoted late. We expected that the successful people studied here would be found to have moved through steadily higher positions, and that the positions would be correlated with one another between successive periods.

Although there are several indicators of professionalism, such as training, self-identification, and group membership, one of the most accessible is education. One study of top U.S. corporate executives found that 43% have graduate degrees, of which 41% are M.B.A.s and 26% are J.D.s (Sussman, 1979, p. 17). The average age of individuals studied by Sussman was 53, and professional education has steadily become more popular in the past two decades; consequently one might anticipate that this measure of professionalism would increase with time among successful individuals (Kotter, 1982, pp. 46-53). It seemed likely that the level of professional standing appropriate to the position would increase throughout a successful person's career; barring sudden shifts in career direction rendering previous professional experiences obsolete, professional standing should, like level, be correlated between periods. Although the prediction seems obvious, some research has found that professional training is unrelated to success among those with the ability to obtain such training, or that the time and money expended in training are not necessarily recaptured (Gordon & Strober, 1978; Pfeffer, 1977; Reder, 1978). Whatever the direct value of professionalism in helping people perform their jobs, however, it may provide a signal to others that the professional is seriously committed to his or her career.

Finally, successful people could be expected to prefer situations having a higher degree of centrality, or central importance to the organization, allowing them to obtain and use power (see Brass, 1985). Although some power can be attained in staff positions (such as human resource management), those positions are usually considered more peripheral, supporting and serving line positions that have authority over what the organization considers its primary activity (see Hitt, Ireland, & Palia, 1982). As one result, staff positions are generally lower paid than line positions (Pfeffer, 1977; Weinstein & Srinivasan, 1974). Consistent with strategic contingencies theory, staff positions are less important to the work flows of the organization and less likely to accumulate power (Hickson, Hinings, Lee, Schneck, & Pennings, 1971; Pfeffer & Moore, 1980). Thus we expected a movement toward line (away from staff) positions by successful people, although again we anticipated that positions would be correlated in successive observation periods.

In summary, movement was expected throughout the careers studied toward increased professional status, line positions, and higher positions. We also anticipated that those studied would show a high degree of consistency (with exceptions as noted below) in

which attainment of a situation on the previous job would correlate
with having the situation in the present job. Finally, we expected
(again, with the exceptions noted below) that attainment of professional status, a line position, and a higher-level position would be
positively associated with hierarchical organizational success.

Sex Differences

A substantial volume of research now exists that demonstrates the
existence of a sexually differentiated labor market (see Davidson &
Cooper, 1983; Larwood & Wood, 1977; Madden, 1985; Nieva and
Gutek, 1981; Olson, Good, & Frieze, 1985; Rosenbaum, 1985). Overall
this work shows that on average, women have lower positions than
men, are paid less in the same position, and are expected to perform
worse under challenging conditions. For example, a 1979 national
survey of 1708 top executives found just eight women in its sample
(Sussman, 1979). A follow-up survey identifying the top 300 women
executives found that they earned an annual average of $24,000 less
than the males studied three years earlier and held substantially lower
positions (Korn/Ferry International, 1982). This research, and hun-
dreds of related studies, indicate that careers of men and women may
proceed quite differently from each other. Women who do not expect
organizational success (whether due to discrimination, differential
socialization, or other factors) might take their jobs more casually,
entering and leaving them more readily than men and ignoring
opportunities for professional training. Similarly, an employer who
expects that women are poorly trained, poorly motivated, unreliable,
or incapable or who feels that others in powerful positions have these
beliefs (whether or not these views are correct) will react by requiring
that those women who are hired accept positions of lower responsibility and by denying them opportunities for the most meaningful
experiences and training (Larwood & Gattiker, 1985; Larwood,
Gutek, & Gattiker, 1984).

The result of these two forces might be that successful women are
systematically delayed, relative to men, in the development of their
careers. If the career development of successful personnel in an
organization is found to be toward higher positions, line operations,
and increased professionalism, as predicted in earlier sections, then
the women may be systematically found in lower positions (relative to

men with the same years of experience), the less important—staff—positions, and positions demanding a lower degree of professional commitment. Such a delay might become increasingly obvious as later jobs are considered and earlier delays are progressively compounded. This suggests that women may be expected to reach the same positions later in their careers than will men but does not predict that women will be kept out of important positions entirely.

Age Cohorts and Social Change

It would be convenient if potential cohort and social change effects could be described separately. With experience-related changes one might anticipate with the classic or neoclassic models of externally unimpeded career development that a younger group would follow essentially the same pattern of development as an otherwise similar older group. For this reason we expected to find that analysis of the situations of younger men would find them seeming to lag behind older men; actually the younger men were expected to be in similar situations to those formerly occupied by the older group when it was younger. The situations of both younger and older men were both expected to be statistically related to hierarchical success, but the levels of success thus far obtained by younger men were anticipated to be lower.

Among women the dual development model seemed to point to quite different results, requiring consideration of both cohort and social change effects. If organizations that had formerly discriminated made an effort to cease discrimination—particularly if they attempted to advance and encourage women—the career patterns of women would seem discontinuous in at least two respects. First, both older and younger women might be similarly affected at the same time without regard for age. For example, an employer's changed behavior in 1975 could affect all women in the organization at the same time irrespective of seniority. Thus the situations held by younger and older women might be indistinguishable from each other. Rosenbaum (1985) found some evidence in this direction in his study of the career progress of men and women in one firm at several points along a twelve-year career path. Generally senior women gained less than younger women from affirmative action, closing the differences between the two groups. Supportive findings were also contained in Bureau of Census statistics reported by Blau and Ferber (1985, p. 43) to the effect that younger women earned 71.8% of salaries of comparable men, whereas older women earned just 55.7%, and by Korn/Ferry International (1982) that their sample of upper-level women was seven years younger than the sample of top male executives. These results might also be anticipated from studies indicating that starting success predicts continued and later success, in part through the Pygmalion effect (Eden & Ravid, 1982; Olson et al., 1985). Thus older women may have already demonstrated failure in the eyes of employers and may thereby have damaged their further potential and neutralized the advantage of experience.

The second change from the career development progression of men might be found in career discontinuities among women: The careers of women might not show smooth relationships between antecedent situations and hierarchical success. In efforts to move women along quickly under pressure of equal opportunity regulations, organizations would not necessarily take the same care to ensure that the women had obtained the background experience expected of men. Women therefore might seem to lack the appropriate preparation but to be moved up irrespective of it. Describing the same effect differently, they might seem to be progressing more randomly than men, while nonetheless progressing, or to be leaping over intermediate steps and thereby reaching successful positions not generally associated with someone having their background. Thus it would be more difficult to describe a woman's successful career than a man's.

Hypotheses

In summary, this study examines six major hypotheses. The first three describe the development of career situations (professional status, line-staff position, level in the department) across several points in time:

Hypothesis 1: The careers of successful people move toward increased professional status, line positions, and higher positions within the department.

Hypothesis 2: Men have higher professional status, are more often in line positions, and have higher levels in their departments than women.

Hypothesis 3: The careers of younger men parallel but lag behind those of older men, whereas the progress of younger women is similar to that of older women.

The final group of hypotheses is concerned with the relationship between the situations previously held and hierarchical success (present position in the department, level in the organization, and achieving officer or director status):

Hypothesis 4: Line, professional, and higher departmental positions are correlated with themselves in successive periods of time and may lead to hierarchical success.

Hypothesis 5: The relationships between successive situations and those between situations and hierarchical success are consistent for men but not for women.

Hypothesis 6: Younger men hold lower levels of hierarchical success than older men. Younger women are indistinguishable in their levels of hierarchical success from older women.

METHOD

Seventeen major corporations were selected at random from a published list of the largest firms operating in California. Human resource officers of these firms were asked to participate in a study of the career paths of their "successful" personnel by distributing questionnaires to sixteen persons whom they believed to be successful. The definition of "successful" was intentionally left open so as not to limit the sample arbitrarily. The personnel officers were each requested to obtain a stratified sample with approximately equal numbers of men and women, line and staff, and younger (under age 40) and older individuals. The individuals nominated then responded anonymously to the researchers.

Of the potential 272 respondents, 215 (79%) completed the survey. Responses were divided for the analyses discussed here into four groups: younger males (n = 52), younger females (n = 64), older males (n = 66), and older females (n = 33). Older women were underrepresented, according to some personnel officers, because there were not enough successful older women in their organizations. The line-staff distinction was requested of participating firms only to ensure that the sample represented both categories of personnel and was not used directly in the analyses reported here.

The 215 participants described their present job and each of those they had previously held by providing the position, department, industry, and effective dates of their employment in each position. Respondents had held an average of 6.9 positions in 3.2 organizations, with no significant differences by sex. Because the number of positions held varied, we analyzed the results selectively by examining careers in four periods: the first job, the third from last, the last job, and the present position. The position descriptions were dummy coded for three variables: professional (a position requiring long-term commitment, training, or specialization) or nonprofessional (a position inconsistent with his or her specialization or not requiring professional commitment); line (dealing directly with and in authority over the core activities of the organization) or staff (supportive) activities; and entry, middle, or high level in the department. Separately, respondents answered a series of questions concerning their present level of success, including the number of levels to the top from their position in their organization and whether they held officer or director status. It should be recognized that professional status included other professions besides management, and that high level in the department is not necessarily the same as high level in the organization. Thus an individual could move upward in the organization while moving from a professional to a nonprofessional position and while moving to a lower position in a more powerful or central department.

Method of Analysis

Hypotheses 1 to 3 predicted patterns of change in the three situation variables: professional/other career status, line/staff department membership, and management level in the department. These were analyzed by means of comparisons both within and between the four sex-age classifications in order to determine whether the predicted patterns of change or similarity over time in professional status, line/staff membership, and management level had occurred. Overall analyses of effect direction were conducted by means of one-tailed sign tests (a nonparametric test appropriate for determining that events occur more often in a predicted direction than would be expected by chance—Bradley, 1968, pp. 164-192); one-tailed t-tests provided individual comparisons between means.

Hypotheses 4 and 5 were concerned with the manner in which early career antecedent conditions lead through later conditions to hierarchical organizational success. Such predictions would usually call for a path analysis, either to determine the statistically "best" path between points or to test the fit of a hypothetical model to the data. Either approach discards some relationship information and assumes a level of theoretical or empirical sophistication that neither the career development nor the sex-role literature yet affords. Furthermore, the "residuals" tend to be correlated with the variables that precede them in our model (e.g., current with previous job), and the variables used were not measured on an interval scale. It has been suggested that these two violations of assumptions in path analysis seriously impede any possible generalizations (Pedhazur, 1982, p. 582). Consequently, we examined Hypotheses 4 and 5 via a naive analytic scheme, with an intercorrelation matrix (Pearson's r), testing all possible interrelationships. In order to keep coincidental relationships to a minimum, we set the alpha level conservatively at .01 (one-tailed) for these analyses. Hypothesis 6, predicting age-related differences in hierarchical success for men but not for women, was again examined by means of t-tests.

RESULTS

Situations

Our first hypothesis predicted that the situations of successful people would develop by their successively obtaining professional status, moving toward line (away from staff) positions, and moving up. Means for the situational variables describing the careers of respondents are shown in Figures 8.1-8.3. A sign test for each variable, visually comparing the mean of each group with the preceding period mean, determined that ten of twelve changes between periods were in the predicted direction for professional status (p < .05 by a one-tailed sign test), eight of twelve were as predicted for the line-staff designation (n.s.), and all twelve were in the expected direction for position in the department ($p < .001$). Similar results appear in Table 8.1, in which means for the first job are compared with those of the present position using t-tests. Each of the four groups moved up significantly in professional status and departmental position between the first and present job, whereas none made significant overall movements with respect to the line/staff measure. Thus the respondents examined here systematically acquired more professional status and moved up in their departments but did not move reliably either out of or into staff positions.

The second hypothesis suggested that women and men would differ with respect to the three situational variables: We anticipated that men would more often have professional status, that men would more often be in line positions, and that men would occupy higher positions within their organizations than women. As expected, the six comparisons of younger men with younger women and older men with older women on each of the three variables (see the differences shown in Figures 8.1-8.3) were each in the predicted direction (overall $p < .05$ by a sign test). The sign test provided an overview of the results; the strength of specific comparisons was again examined using follow-up t-tests comparing males and females in the same age group in the present job. Despite all differences being in the predicted direction, only four of the six t-test comparisons were statistically significant: those between older men and women and that for the department-level variable between younger men and women (Table 8.1).

Hypothesis 3 posited that the careers of younger men would lag behind those of older men in development, whereas the careers of younger and older women would not differ markedly from each other. Because respondents were approximately the same age at the time of their first positions, only third from last, last, and present positions could be used for this analysis. In support of the first part of the hypothesis, means for younger men showed lower levels of professional status, less line authority, and lower department position than for older men in all nine comparisons ($p < .01$ by a sign test of the nine comparisons taken together). Five of the nine subsequent t-tests comparing younger with older men on the three career measures at the three points in time were individually significant. Among women only three of the nine comparisons found that older women had greater professional status, more line authority, or higher

Table 8.1
Situations and Hierarchical Success of Men and Women

	1 Younger Men			2 Younger Women			3 Older Men			4 Older Women			t-Test Comparisons Between Groups					
Time Period	X	S.D.	N	X	S.D.	N	X	S.D.	N	X	S.D.	N	1.2 t	1.3 t	1.4 t	2.3 t	2.4 t	3.4 t
Professional Status																		
First job	1.317	.471	41	1.628	.488	51	1.436	.500	55	1.680	.476	25	3.110**		3.114**			2.235*
Third from last job	1.361	.487	36	1.435	.501	46	1.097	.298	52	1.429	.507	21		3.067**		4.059**		3.411**
Last job	1.200	.404	50	1.293	.459	58	1.033	.181	60	1.300	.466	30		2.798**		4.048**		3.583**
Present job	1.135	.345	52	1.219	.417	64	1.064	.246	63	1.267	.450	30				2.551*		2.699**
T first vs. present job	2.114*			4.811**			5.128**			3.276**								
Line/Staff																		
First job	1.415	.499	41	1.660	.478	50	1.400	.494	55	1.720	.458	25	2.392*			2.741**		3.004**
Third from last job	1.500	.507	36	1.578	.500	45	1.423	.499	52	1.524	.512	21						
Last job	1.480	.505	50	1.655	.480	58	1.367	.486	60	1.667	.480	30	1.846*		1.698*	3.239**		2.946**
Present job	1.462	.503	52	1.562	.500	64	1.270	.447	63	1.600	.498	30		2.164*		3.469**		3.363**
T first vs. present job																		
Position in Department																		
First job	1.146	.358	41	1.060	.240	50	1.091	.348	55	1.000	.000	25				2.342*		1.654*
Third from last job	1.750	.770	36	1.200	.404	45	1.904	.721	52	1.143	.478	21	4.025**		3.576**	5.932**		5.315**
Last job	2.040	.755	50	1.702	.706	57	2.533	.623	60	1.667	.661	30	2.392*	3.735**	2.351**	6.750**		6.396**
Present job	2.404	.748	52	2.141	.774	64	2.794	.446	63	2.167	.699	30	1.861*	3.396**		5.825**		5.156**
T first vs. present job	10.289**			10.071**			23.123**			8.675**								
Additional Hierarchical Success Measures																		
Level in organization	2.923	2.047	52	3.203	2.033	64	2.106	1.764	66	2.909	2.350	33		2.322*		3.286**		1.923*
Officer or director	1.628	.488	51	1.703	.460	64	1.400	.494	65	1.625	.492	32		2.501**		3.605**		2.247*

Note. Item scaling is as follows: Professional status (professional [1] to other [2]); Line position (line [1] to staff [2]) to staff in department (entry to top [3]); Level in organization (no levels between respondent and top [0] to nine levels between self and top [9]); and Officer or director (officer or director [1] to other [2]).

*p < .05; **p < .01 by a one-tail t-test of the difference means indicated. Only statistically significant results are reported.

141

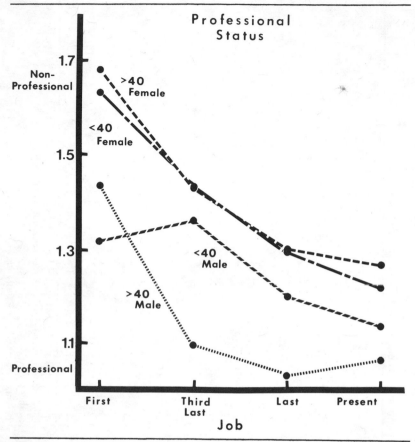

Figure 8.1. Professional status in four time periods.

departmental position than younger women (n.s. by a sign test); none of the nine t-tests was individually significant. Although it is difficult to demonstrate a null hypothesis predicting no differences by age among women, this nonetheless provides some evidence supporting that proposition.

Hierarchical Success

Hypotheses 4 and 5 concerned the manner in which the measures discussed earlier lead to hierarchical success. Hierarchical success was

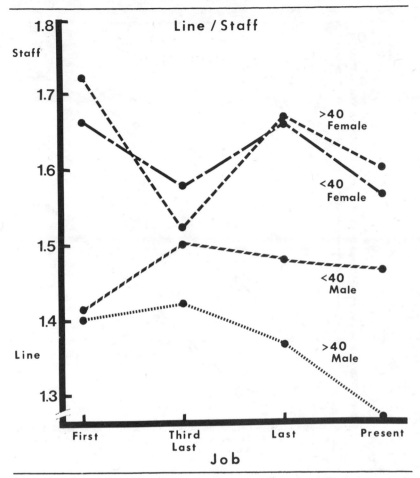

Figure 8.2. Line-staff position in four time periods.

measured by three variables: levels between one's own position and the top of the organization, whether the respondent had obtained officer or director status by the time of the study, and his or her present level within the department. Thus level within the department was used in this section in two ways: For each period it was used as an indicator of situational development; for the present period it was also a measure of hierarchical success.

The fourth hypothesis predicted that professional, line, and higher department level situations lead to later hierarchical success. Figures

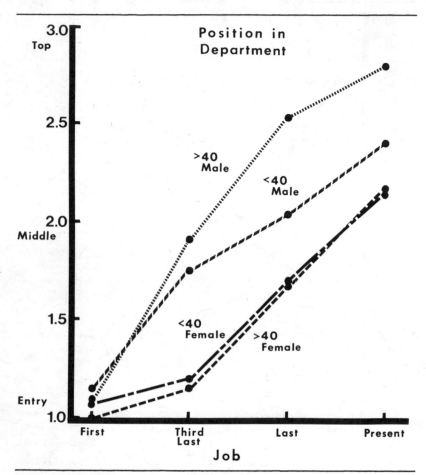

Figure 8.3. Position in department in four time periods.

8.4-8.7 show all correlational relationships among the situational and hierarchical success variables reaching $p < .01$ or better for the four respondent groups. Variable scaling is provided to the left of the figures. In addition, means, group sizes, and standard deviations for all variables appear in Table 8.1. Inspection of the figure shows that present level in the department is significantly linked with immediate prior level and with level in the organization for all four groups. For the two male groups and for the older female group, higher present level in the department was also linked with officer status. None of the situational variables reliably predicted officer or director status for younger women.

Line and professional situations were not as closely linked to hierarchical success as was level within the department. For younger males, however, holding a line (as compared with a staff) position was consistent with having a higher position in the organization (fewer levels to the top); for older males, line positions were related to officer status. Professional status correlated with higher department level for younger women but higher organizational level for younger men.

These results support our prediction that line, professional, and high positions are linked with hierarchical success. Not all relationships were significant; nonetheless, all of those reaching significance were in the direction predicted ($p < .001$ by a two-tailed sign test of the direction of the significant relationships). The results indicate that each of the situational variables is potentially important. Further, given that the links between the same situation measured in successive periods are among the outstanding features of Figures 8.4-8.7, the earlier an individual can attain professional status and reach the upper level of a line department, the more likely he or she is to achieve hierarchical success. Still, nothing can be regarded as guaranteed: There were no reliable direct links between the earliest job situations and present success.

Hypothesis 5 predicted that the route to success is consistent for men but not for women. Comparison of the figures for men and women at each of the two age groups provides evidence in support of this expectation. For older men we found that high department level in the first position was related, through successive links, to hierarchical success. For older women there was no such entry point. Early high department position for the older women was statistically irrelevant. Line status on the first job (which correlated directly with line status in the present period) seemed important but proved deceptive. Line positions were not statistically associated with hierarchical success for older women as they were for men. In fact, an early line position for older women was *inversely* related to professional status (a situational variable found positively associated with hierarchical success among older men above). Thus it appears that line status was, and still is, irrelevant to older women's hierarchical success.

Among younger male respondents all three situational variables in the first job were statistically related to the same measures at later

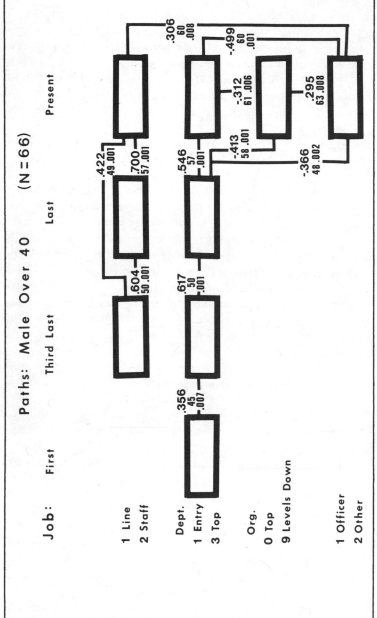

Job: First   Third Last   Last   Present   Paths: Male Over 40   (N = 66)

Figure 8.4. Career development of older males. Figures between boxes are Pearson's r, degrees of freedom, and probability (one-tailed) for relationships between boxes; all correlations beyond .01 are given. Means in boxes appear in Table 8.1.

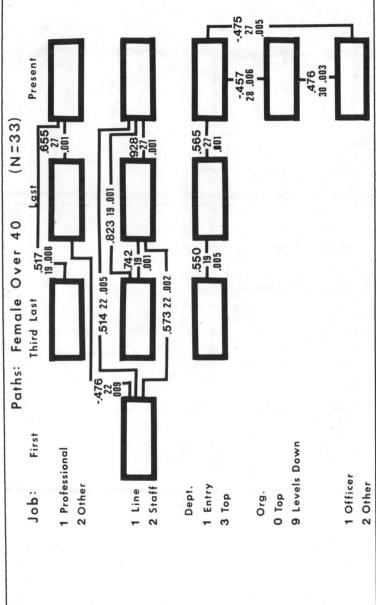

Figure 8.5. Career development of older females. Figures between boxes are Pearson's r, degrees of freedom, and probability (one-tailed) for relationships between boxes; all correlations beyond .01 are given. Means in boxes appear in Table 8.1.

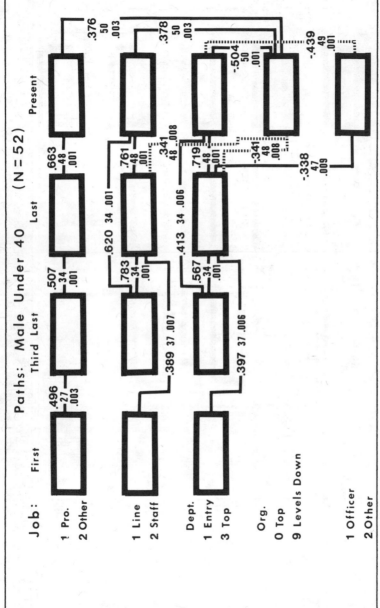

Figure 8.6. Career development of younger males. Figures between boxes are Pearson's r, degrees of freedom, and probability (one-tailed) for relationships between boxes; all correlations beyond .01 are given. Means in boxes appear in Table 8.1.

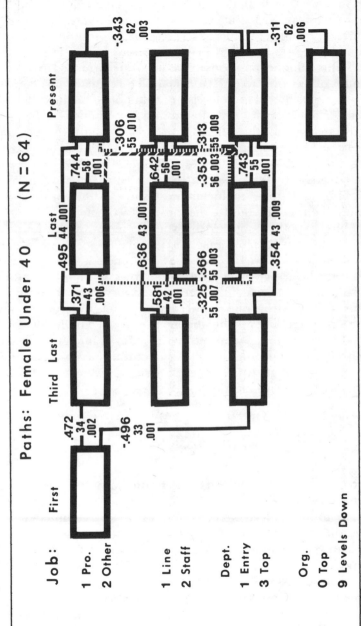

Figure 8.7. Career development of younger females. Figures between boxes are Pearson's r, degrees of freedom, and probability (one-tailed) for relationships between boxes; all correlations beyond .01 are given. Means in boxes appear in Table 8.1.

149

points in time. As well, all three of the situational variables in the last or present job predicted at least one of the hierarchical success measures. For younger women, however, only professional status on the first job led statistically to later situations (either later professional status or higher positions in the department) related to success. Although officer or director status could be predicted for younger men who had achieved high levels, it could not be predicted for the women. As noted earlier, although a null hypothesis is difficult to demonstrate, we take the difference in career patterns for men and women as evidence supporting Hypothesis 5. At least on the basis of the measures used in this study, it was possible to track the progress in men's careers, showing how first jobs related eventually, through intervening situations, to hierarchical success; this process was substantially more tenuous for the careers of women.

Our final hypothesis asserted that younger men would be found to differ significantly from older men in their achievement of hierarchical success, whereas younger and older women would not differ significantly from each other. The bottom rows of Table 8.1 confirm this prediction. For each of the three success measures, younger and older men differed from one another at $p < .05$ or better; younger and older women were not reliably different from one another ($t < 1.0$, n.s.). With respect to the same means, it is also of interest that older women enjoyed significantly less hierarchical success than older men, whereas younger women's levels of success were not meaningfully below those of younger men.

DISCUSSION

This research has examined some limited aspects of the career development of successful personnel in major corporations. Our emphases in the analysis were twofold. First, we were interested in determining movement toward three situational variables: professional status, line positions, and higher departmental levels. Second, we expected to find that the situational variables were related to hierarchical success in the organization.

Our findings substantially supported predictions made on the basis of career development, sex role, and organizational behavior literatures. The four groups examined (younger and older men and women) increased their professional standing and level in their department between their first and present job. Unexpectedly, they did not move toward line and away from staff positions. Overall, men had greater professional standing, were more often in line positions, and were higher in their departments than women—however, the effect was primarily confined to older rather than to younger men. Although the younger men appeared to be following (lagging behind) the older men, younger and older women did not differ from each other in their situations across time.

Regarding hierarchical success, the results indicated that each of the situational variables can lead progressively toward higher positions in the department at the present time, higher organizational positions, and officer or director status. Nonetheless, as anticipated, the progression appears less regular for women than for men. For instance, younger men could apply professional standing, line positions, or higher department levels in the first job in the service of attaining eventual hierarchical success, whereas younger women could systematically benefit only from professional status on the first job and had no consistent means to attain officer or director status. Finally, older women had attained lower levels on the hierarchical success than older men; younger men and women were not significantly different from each other.

Theoretical Implications

How should these results be interpreted? At their most basic level they corroborate earlier findings that early success, such as attaining a high position in the department, is helpful to later hierarchical success (Berlew & Hall, 1976; Eden & Ravid, 1982; Olson et al., 1985). Similarly, professional standing and line status appear to be worthwhile in leading to later success. The results also show that one career position is correlated with later positions; progressive development is the rule, but sudden jumps are the exception (Rosenbaum, 1984). Finally, we have found evidence implying (but not proving) sex discrimination. Older women were significantly behind older men in their hierarchical success. Nonetheless, this might be anticipated from the women's lower levels of development in the antecedent conditions, and the study can imply but not directly determine the reason for those lower levels.

The pattern of results by age and by sex supports a deeper and more interesting analysis. Rather than view the career development of women as similar to that of men, the dual development model offered in the introduction suggests that there can be substantial differences between men's and women's career development. Certainly one of these differences is the historical existence of widespread sex discrimination in organizations (Larwood & Gattiker, 1985; Larwood & Wood, 1977; Madden, 1985). Based on the results of earlier research such as that of Rosenbaum (1985), however, we have argued that there may now be an age context for some organizational sex discrimination. That is, although women's careers may have previously been kept from success, those in decision-making positions may now be selectively pushing some women ahead to fill equal opportunity regulation requirements. This does not imply that the women are any less deserving than the men, however, as they may still be only partly compensated for past discrimination.

In light of the fact that older women will have been previously passed over for some opportunities, and given that late promotion may unfavorably bias subsequent promotion (Rosenbaum, 1984), the effect of efforts at equal opportunity may be to move a small number of younger women ahead more vigorously than older women. A second effect is to move women ahead irregularly, rather than gradually and systematically, as seems more common with men. For the women moved ahead there were fewer commonsense career entry points, such as a high initial department position, of the type from which men launch successful careers. The success of younger women does not say that discrimination is ended, however. Older women are still substantially behind older men, whereas younger women are nonsignificantly behind younger men. Instead, the pattern may indicate that external forces outside her control are more important to a woman's success in her career than to a man's success in his.

Although the dual development model of careers is supported, one cannot regard it as demonstrated. The present study applied the model, which suggested that men and women might be subjected to different social forces and thus that they could have different normative patterns of career development, but did not test it. A test comparing the model with others is still needed. Until then there remain a number of viable alternatives that may explain the age-sex findings. One such possibility is that an internal explanation is adequate (the neoclassic model): Perhaps older women never intended to make organizational careers, but younger women are attempting to succeed and are applying different organizational strategies in the service of their goals (see Larwood & Kaplan, 1980; Larwood,

Radford, & Berger, 1980). Alternatively, the results may be an artifact of the stratified sampling technique, which required that some participating firms include the entire population of older women but which allowed greater selectivity with the other three groups. Further research is needed concerning these limitations.

As a final theoretical note, the term "model" is far too grandiose to be satisfyingly applied to the dual development notion—or to the other concepts of career development discussed in the introduction. "Model" implies the existence of a mechanism hypothetically linking formal variables. Only the vaguest outlines of these models are yet present. It would be useful to set out explicitly the full range of anticipated relationships using each model so that their predictions can be adequately tested and compared.

Practical Implications for
Management and Managerial Careers

At the organizational level, the results indicate that women are moving up less predictably than men. The results may partly refect the application of affirmative action procedures and sensitivity to equal employment opportunity needs. Whatever their source, the findings are fertile ground for intraorganizational research: they allow firms to test directly for the first time what is really needed for top personnel to function successfully. If the women (both younger and older) function successfully without having held the same positions as those held by successful men, it would seem that the traditional career ladder is superfluous. The latter would then be a rite of passage designed to hold back promising personnel until those ahead of them vacate key positions. If this is found, then younger men as well as younger women might benefit as the best might be moved ahead without need of prior experience and preparation. Conversely, a finding that those moved ahead more quickly are not able to function as well would indicate that the career ladder is needed, that the most aggressive affirmative action programs at high levels in the organization are counterproductive, and that some of the women who have been prematurely advanced (relative to men) may have difficulty later in their careers.

If later research were to demonstrate that a portion of the present results is an artifact of the sampling technique in which human resource directors selected participants who seemed (to them) successful, a third possibility exists: Women may be more difficult than men for men to evaluate. Women may be moved ahead more randomly than men because it is difficult for those evaluating them to determine their performance; sex and sex role may overwhelm subtle subjective performance discriminations, and affirmative action may be sufficient to move a few women ahead without other compelling reasons for doing so. Thus the wrong women may be moving ahead for the wrong reasons, such as attractiveness, personality, and loyalty, while more capable women are left behind. In fact, this might set the stage for later failure in which the requirements imposed on women for movement through middle ranks, such as attractiveness, are irrelevant for promotion to the highest positions, where job performance is more closely scrutinized. If this possibility holds, firms would do well to reexamine their employee evaluation systems.

The findings offer some career suggestions at a practical level for those interested in developing organizational careers. Careers for older men and women may already be set and difficult to alter. Although there is no evidence in this study, those who are older but not yet successful may be best advised to shift to another organization where their previous history of slow or late ascent cannot be held against them. For those starting their careers, however, the most useful advice for men interested in hierarchical success would seem to be to start at as high a level as possible in the department, take a line position, and become a professional. For young women the parallel advice is quite simply to become a professional first, and acquire top department positions when possible—and hope for the best.

REFERENCES

Backman, C. W., & Secord, P. F. (1968). The self in role selection. In C. Gordon & K. J. Gergen (Eds.), *The self in social interaction*. New York: John Wiley.

Bem, D. J. (1972). Self-perception theory. In L. Berkowitz (Ed.), *Advances in experimental social psychology* (Vol. 6). New York: Academic Press.

Berlew, D. E., & Hall, D. T. (1976). The socialization of managers: Effects of expectations on performance. *Administrative Science Quarterly, 11*, 207-223.

Biddle, B. J. (1979). *Role theory: Expectations, identities, and behaviors*. New York: Academic Press.

Blau, F. D., & Ferber, M. A. (1985). Women in the labor market: The last twenty years. In L. Larwood, A. H. Stromberg, & B. A. Gutek (Eds.), *Women and work* (Vol. 1, pp. 19-49). Beverly Hills, CA: Sage.

Bradley, J. V. (1968). *Distribution-free statistical tests.* Englewood Cliffs, NJ: Prentice-Hall.

Brass, D. J. (1985). Men's and women's networks: A study of interaction patterns and influence in an organization. *Academy of Management Journal, 28,* 327-343.

Brooks, L. (1984). Counseling special groups: Women and ethnic minorities. In D. Brown, L. Brooks, and Associates (Eds.), *Career choice and development.* San Francisco: Jossey-Bass.

Davidson, M., & Cooper, C. (1983). *Stress and the woman manager.* New York: St. Martin's.

Eden, D., & Ravid, G. (1982). Pygmalion versus self-expectancy: Effects of instructor and self-expectancy on trainee performance. *Organizational Behavior and Human Performance, 30,* 351-364.

Flango, V. E., & Brumbaugh, R. B. (1974). The dimensionality of the cosmopolitan-local construct. *Administrative Science Quarterly, 1974, 19,* 198-210.

Gordon, F., & Strober, M. (1978). Initial observation in a pioneer cohort: 1974 women MBAs. *Sloan Management Review, 20,* 15-23.

Gutteridge, T. G., & Otte, F. L. (1983). *Organizational career development: State of the practice.* Washington, DC: ASTD Press.

Hall, D. T. (1976). *Careers in organizations.* Santa Monica, CA: Goodyear.

Hickson, D. J., Hinings, C. R., Lee, C. A., Schneck, R. E., & Pennings, J. M. (1971). A strategic contingencies' theory of intraorganizational power. *Administrative Science Quarterly, 16,* 216-229.

Hitt, M. A., Ireland, R. D., & Palia, K. A. (1982). Industrial firms' grand strategy and functional importance: Moderating effects of technology and uncertainty. *Academy of Management Journal, 25,* 265-298.

Korman, A. K. (1976). Hypothesis of work behavior revisited and an extension. *Academy of Management Review, 1,* 50-63.

Korn/Ferry International. (1982). *Korn/Ferry International's survey of women senior executives.* New York: Author.

Kotter, J. P. (1982). *The general managers.* New York: Free Press.

Larwood, L., & Gattiker, U. E. (1985). Rational bias and interorganizational power in the employment of management consultants. *Group & Organization Studies, 10,* 3-18.

Larwood, L., Gutek, B. A., & Gattiker, U. E. (1984). Perspectives on institutional discrimination and resistance to change. *Group & Organization Studies, 9,* 333-352.

Larwood, L., & Kaplan, M. (1980). Job tactics of women in banking. *Group & Organization Studies, 5,* 70-79.

Larwood, L., Radford, L. M. & Berger, D. (1980). Do job tactics predict success? A comparison of female with male executives in 14 corporations. *Academy of Management Proceedings,* 386-390.

Larwood, L., & Wood, M. M. (1977). *Women in management.* Lexington, MA: D. C. Heath.

London, M., & Stumpf, S. A. (1982). *Managing careers.* Reading, MA: Addison-Wesley.

Lopez, E. M. (1982). A test of the self-consistency theory of the job performance-job satisfaction relationship. *Academy of Management Journal, 25,* 335-348.

Madden, J. F. (1985). The persistence of pay differentials: The economics of sex discrimination. In L. Larwood, A. H. Stromberg, & B. A. Gutek (Eds.), *Women and work* (Vol. 1, pp. 76-114). Beverly Hills, CA: Sage.

Nieva, V. F., & Gutek, B. A. (1981). *Women and work: A psychological perspective.* New York: Praeger.

Olson, J. E., Good, D. C., & Frieze, I. H. (1985). *Income differentials of male and female MBAs: The effects of job type and industry.* Paper presented at 1985 annual meeting of the Academy of Management, San Diego.

Osipow, S. H. (1983). *Theories of career development* (3rd ed.). Englewood Cliffs, NJ: Prentice-Hall.

Pedhazur, E. H. (1982). *Multiple regression in behavioral research* (2nd ed.). New York: CBS College Publishing.

Pfeffer, J. (1977). Effects of an MBA and socioeconomic origins on business school graduates' salaries. *Journal of Applied Psychology, 62,* 698-705.

Pfeffer, J., & Moore, W. L. (1980). Power in university budgeting: A replication and extension. *Administrative Science Quarterly, 25,* 637-653.

Raelin, J. A. (1982). A comparative analysis of female-male early youth careers. *Industrial Relations, 21,* 231-247.

Reder, M. W. (1978). An analysis of a closely observed labor market. Starting salaries for University of Chicago MBAs. *Journal of Business, 16,* 263-297.

Rosenbaum, J. E. (1984). *Career mobility in a corporate hierarchy.* Orlando, FL: Academic Press.

Rosenbaum, J. E. (1985). Persistence and change in pay inequalities: Implications for job evaluation and comparable worth. In L. Larwood, A. H. Stromberg, & B. A. Gutek (Eds.), *Women and work* (Vol. 1, pp. 115-140). Beverly Hills, CA: Sage.

Schein, E. H. (1971). The individual, the organization, and the career: A conceptual scheme. *Journal of Applied Behavioral Science, 7,* 401-426.

Schein, E. H. (1978). *Career dynamics.* Reading, MA: Addison-Wesley.

Souerwine, A. H. (1978). *Career strategies: Planning for personal achievement.* New York: AMACOM.

Spenner, K. I., Otto, L. B., & Call, V. R. A. (1982). *Career lines and careers.* Lexington, MA: D. C. Heath.

Stewart, L. P., & Gudykunst, W. B. (1982). Differential factors influencing the hierarchical level and number of promotions of males and females within an organization. *Academy of Management Journal, 25,* 586-597.

Sussman, J. A. (1979). *Korn/Ferry International's executive profile: A survey of corporate leaders.* New York: Korn/Ferry International.

Tedeschi, J. T., Schlenker, B. R., & Bonoma, T. V. (1971). Cognitive dissonance: Private ratiocination or public spectacle? *American Psychologist, 26,* 685-695.

Weiner, Y., & Vaitenas, R. (1977). Personality correlates of voluntary midcareer change in enterprising occupations. *Journal of Applied Psychology, 62,* 706-712.

Weinstein, A. G., & Srinivasan, V. (1974). Predicting managerial success of master of business administration (MBA) candidates. *Journal of Applied Psychology, 59,* 207-212.

9

Family Roles
A Help or a Hindrance for Working Women?

ROBERTA L. VALDEZ and BARBARA A. GUTEK

Data gathered in a representative survey of 827 employed women in Los Angeles County were used to test the contradictory predictions supported by the theories of role conflict and role accumulation about the effects of the work-family relationship for women. The two theories have different implications for women's careers. Some of the findings were consistent with a role conflict explanation of the relationship of work and family for women; others were supportive of role accumulation theory. For the findings that a larger than expected proportion of women with managerial positions are divorced or separated and that as the level of commitment and preparation required for a job rises, there is an increase in the proportion of childless women and a decrease in the proportion with three or more children under age 18, a role conflict conceptualization is useful. The findings related to job satisfaction and familial circumstances provide support for a role accumulation explanation. It was found that the lowest levels of job dissatisfaction were found among married or cohabiting women, and lower levels of job satisfaction were found among the never married.

A large body of evidence has accumulated indicating the interdependence of work and family life (Chacko, 1983; Cooke & Rousseau, 1984; Gutek, Nakamura, & Nieva, 1981; Near, Rice, & Hunt, 1980; Pleck, Staines, & Lang, 1980), an interdependence especially problematic for women workers as a result of their greater family

responsibilities. Women have traditionally had the primary responsibility for housekeeping and child care, and these household
responsibilities do not diminish for women when they are employed
outside the home (Angrist, Lave, & Mickelsen, 1976; Bryson, Bryson,
& Johnson, 1978; Nieva & Gutek, 1981).

Moreover, because women bear the primary responsibility for
child care, their work and family demands are simultaneous, whereas
those experienced by men are more typically sequential (Hall, 1972).
That is, a woman may be called at work regarding a sick child
(simultaneous demands), whereas unless the demands are urgent, the
father can fulfill role obligations after work hours (sequential
demands). Not only are the demands of the family allowed to intrude
into work role more than vice versa for women, but given situations
requiring a choice between the two roles, the family will often take
priority (Pleck, 1977).

These very real demands are bound to affect women's careers. Laws
(1979) contends that marriage and children affect a woman's career
opportunities and progress more than work affects her family life.
Evidence is supportive of this contention; in addition, it has been
found that although employers and others view marriage and
children as a burden or hindrance for a woman's career, they are
regarded as assets to a man's career (Bryson et al., 1978; Bronstein,
Black, Pfennig, & White, this volume).

The trends in the labor force participation of women make it
especially important to understand better the work-family dynamics
for women. It is projected that in the years ahead the greatest addition
in the labor force will be among married women between the ages of
25 and 54, with a 56% increase in participation of those with children
under 18 (Smith, 1979).

Two theories, role conflict and role accumulation, support different predictions about the effects of the work-family interaction for
women. Hall (1972) suggests that chronic role conflict, defined as
mutually competing demands and expectancies by role senders, exists
for many working women as a consequence of the demanding and
pervasive nature of women's home and family roles. Consistent with
this perspective, working women perceive greater interrole conflict
and overload than either men or nonemployed women (Hall &
Gordon, 1973; Herman & Gyllstrom, 1977; Keith & Schafer, 1980).

Professional women and dual-career families have been the topic of much research, and work and family role conflicts have been well documented for this group (Gray, 1983; Heckman, Bryson, & Bryson, 1977; Rapoport & Rapoport, 1971). Evidence suggests that marriage may be seen as incompatible with a career highly demanding of time and commitment (Herman & Gyllstrom, 1977; Mueller & Campbell, 1977; Rosow & Rose, 1972), and other findings indicate that parenthood is consistently seen as conflict arousing for professional women (Beckman, 1978; Bryson et al., 1978; Johnson & Johnson, 1977; St. John-Parsons, 1978).

Both marital status and family size have been shown to be related to reactions to work, such as job satisfaction (Near et al., 1980). Much of the evidence concerning the effects of family situation on the job satisfaction of working women is consistent with a role conflict explanation. In several studies, married women, single parents, and those with children under age 6 have been shown to be appreciably less satisfied with their jobs than other women (Andrisiani & Shapiro, 1978; Gutek et al., 1981).

According to the role accumulation theory proposed by Sieber (1974), the conflict and overload arising from having a multiplicity of roles can be overshadowed by the rewards of role accumulation. In addition to the privileges, resources, and enhancement of the self-concept that accrue from having many roles, Sieber suggested that role strain might be compensated for by buffers against failure that multiple roles provide; if one fails in one sphere or relationship, one has others to fall back on. Hence the net result would be a positive experience for the individual.

Although role accumulation theory per se has been subjected to much less investigation than role conflict theory, some of the social support research explores the effects of multiple roles. In that literature marriage has been shown to mitigate the effects of stress and undesirable life events on a variety of physical and mental health outcomes (Gove, 1973; LaRocco, House, & French, 1980; Thoits, 1982; Verbrugge, 1983). In a study that is particularly relevant to the present inquiry, Cooke and Rousseau (1984) investigated both the role theory prediction that multiple roles can lead to interrole conflict and, consequently, physical and psychological strain, and the social support theory prediction that family roles (i.e., spouse, parent) can reduce strain. The researchers found that family roles were indirectly and positively related to psychological strain (i.e., job and life dissatisfaction) through their relationship to interrole conflict (which was positively associated with increased work-role expectations and number of family roles) but directly and negatively related to physical strain.

Crosby's (1982) findings, however, are supportive of role accumulation theory with respect to the effect of family roles on job satisfaction. Crosby found that single people were less positive about their jobs than married people or parents, and concluded that "for married workers and especially for parents, the joys of home may wash away the concerns and smooth away the disgruntlements of the office, the factory, or the shop. Perhaps, too, some of the woes of parenthood . . . may put difficulties at work in a new, rather soft light" (p. 74).

The purpose of the current study is to test the predictions the two theories support about the effects of the work-family interaction for women. Because much of the research on working women is limited to certain occupational groups—particularly professional women—this study has the advantage of examining many different combinations of work and family life to understand better the interaction, a need suggested by both Appelbaum (1981) and Gutek et al. (1981).

The first prediction examined concerns the comparison of marital status and number of children of working women across occupations. Given that one method of alleviating role strain is to limit or eliminate roles (Goode, 1960; Herman & Gyllstrom, 1977), it is expected on the basis of role conflict theory that women in professional- or managerial-level jobs will differ from other employed women in terms of familial circumstances, given the high demands of those jobs. It was anticipated that those with jobs requiring above-average preparation and commitment are more likely to be unmarried or divorced and have fewer children than clerical, sales, unskilled, and service workers.

If, as suggested by role accumulation theory, the strains associated with combined marital, and/or parental, and work responsibilities can be compensated for by the advantages associated with multiple roles, then it is expected that professional and managerial women will be no more likely to be divorced or to have fewer children than other occupational groups. Because job satisfaction has been demonstrated to be related to familial circumstances for women, this relationship was assessed across occupations to test the predictions supported by each theory. On the basis of role conflict theory it was anticipated that those women with the greatest potential for conflict and overload (i.e., married women and/or those with children under 18) will report lower levels of job satisfaction than women with less potential for conflict. A contradictory prediction is consistent with the theory of role accumulation given that additional roles provide buffers against job-related strains.

METHOD

Subjects

The data were gathered in a representative telephone survey of working adults in Los Angeles County conducted in 1980. In order to be included in the survey, the respondents had to have been at least 18 years of age, been currently employed outside the home 20 or more hours a week, and have been employed for the previous three months. There were 827 women and 405 men, for a total of 1232 respondents, in the final sample, with women oversampled (see Gutek, 1985, for a description of the sampling strategy). The sample of 827 women, representative of working women in Los Angeles County in 1980, was used for the analyses reported in this chapter.

Variables

Questions covered in the interview included (1) characteristics of the respondent's job, (2) the respondent's experience with social-sexual behaviors on the job, and (3) demographic characteristics of the respondent. For the current study the variables of interest included occupation, job satisfaction, number of children under 18, marital status, and age.

Occupation was recorded using three-digit Census Bureau codes, and the occupational categories of "professional," "managerial," "clerical and skilled," "semi- and unskilled," and "service workers" were derived according to the bureau's grouping of occupations (see Quinn & Staines, 1979). The question, "How satisfied are you with your current job?" was used to assess job satisfaction. Respondents were given four response choices ranging from "very satisfied" to "very dissatisfied." Although scales are often preferred for minimizing error variance, Scarpello and Campbell (1983), in their study of several measures of job satisfaction, reported that not only were single-item measures *not* unreliable, but they found that a 1-5 global rating was a more inclusive measure of overall job satisfaction than summation of many facet responses. Andrisiani and Shapiro (1978) also found support for the construct validity of a single-item measure of job satisfaction.

The demographic variables of age, marital status, and number of children under 18 were measured by standard single-item questions. Responses to the marital status question were combined to yield three categories: "currently married or cohabiting," "widowed, divorced or separated," and "never married."

Data Analysis

Log-linear analysis, which provides a means for examining relationships in multidimensional contingency tables, was the primary method of data analysis. This method, by means of a sequential modeling process, allows the determination of which relationships (e.g., two-way and higher-order interactions) are necessary and sufficient to reproduce the observed cell frequencies (Dixon, 1981; Hayes, 1981). Using the maximum likelihood ratio chi-square statistic, the goodness of fit between cell frequencies expected under a given model and those observed is assessed. Simple models that fit the data are contrasted with hierarchically more complex models to obtain the "best-fitting" model. The preferred model is the most parsimonious one that fits the data and is not improved upon significantly by more complex models (Lemkau & Pottick, in press).

Log-linear analysis has important advantages over traditional two-way contingency tables analysis (chi-square). First, it provides a means for assessing the significance of interactions when all of the main effects and other interactions are considered, which is not possible with independent chi-square analyses. It also allows relationships among variables to emerge that might otherwise not be discovered by other means of data analysis.

The first research question was addressed by examining the relationships among the variables occupation, marital status, number of children, and age of the respondent. The other research question was investigated using those variables as well as job satisfaction. Age was included in the analyses so that its effect could be controlled in interpreting significant effects.

Traditional two-way contingency table analysis (chi-square) was employed to clarify bivariate relationships that were found significant in the multivariate contingency table analyses. Analysis of variance with a priori contrasts was also used to examine the relationship of job satisfaction and familial circumstances for each occupational category. For the purposes of those analyses, a variable representing the various possible combinations of marital status and number of children was created.

RESULTS

Familial Circumstances Across Occupations

In comparing familial circumstances across occupations, log-linear analysis using the variables occupation, marital status, number of children, and age revealed that a model with higher-order interactions did not fit the data better than a simpler model with single bivariate relationships. The bivariate relationships included in the best model that are relevant to the predictions of this study were the occupation and marital status interaction, and the occupation and number of children interaction.

The prediction, based on role conflict theory, that women in high-status jobs would be more likely to be divorced was partially supported. As with the sample as a whole, the greatest proportion of women with professional and managerial jobs were married or cohabiting. However, a larger than expected proportion of women with managerial jobs were widowed, divorced, or separated (see Table 9.1).

This is especially noteworthy considering the fact that a larger proportion of managerial workers are in the 36-45-year age category than in the other occupational categories (32% compared with 22.3%, 20%, and 25%), and that this age group has the highest proportion of married women of any of the age groups (65.2% compared with 36.4%, 52.5%, and 59.2%).

Table 9.1
Relationship of Marital Status and Occupation for Women
(percentages)

Occupation	Married or Cohabiting	Widowed, Divorced, Separated	Never Married	Total	n
Professional	61.0	20.0	19.0	100	205
Managerial	53.8	36.9	9.2	100	65
Clerical and skilled	48.6	25.3	26.1	100	403
Semiskilled and unskilled	70.0	18.3	11.7	100	60
Service	50.0	23.3	26.7	100	86

χ^2 (8, N = 819) = 26.5, p < .001.

Based on role conflict theory, it was also anticipated that women professionals and managers would have fewer children than those in lower-status jobs. The pattern of results provides support for this hypothesis. As the level of commitment and preparation required for a job rises, there is a general decrease in the proportion of women with three or more children and a general increase in the proportion of childless women (see Table 9.2).

Occupation, Family, and Job Satisfaction

To address the research question regarding the relationships between job satisfaction and familial circumstances, log-linear analysis with the variables of occupation, marital status, number of children, age, and job satisfaction was used. The best model included the eight two-way interactions. (Higher-order interactions were not necessary for best model fitting.) The most relevant for current purposes was the job satisfaction and marital status interaction.

The prediction, based on role conflict theory, that women with the greatest potential for conflict and overload (i.e., married women and/or those with children under 18) would report lower levels of job satisfaction was not supported. However, although the women in the sample taken as a whole reported themselves more satisfied than dissatisfied, as has been found in past research assessing satisfaction (Gutek, 1978), the group with the smallest proportion expressing dissatisfaction was married women. Also, whereas 52% of married women and 50% of widowed, divorced, or separated women indicate

Table 9.2
Relationship of Occupation and Number of
Children for Women (percentages)

Occupation	No Children	1 or 2 Children	3 or More Children	Total	n
Professional	65.0	27.2	7.8	100	206
Managerial	63.1	30.8	6.2	100	65
Clerical and skilled	63.8	29.8	6.5	100	403
Semiskilled and unskilled	45.0	45.0	10.0	100	60
Service	54.7	30.2	15.1	100	86

χ^2 (8, N = 820) = 16.4, p < .04.

that they are very satisfied with their jobs, only 41% of never-married women make that indication (see Table 9.3).

Interestingly, even though previous research has indicated that marriage and parenthood may be more conflict producing for those with jobs that are highly demanding of time and commitment, three-way interactions did not make a significant contribution to the model. ANOVAs using a combined marital status and number of children variable by job satisfaction for each occupation were nonsignificant as well.

DISCUSSION

Some of the findings of the present study are consistent with a role conflict explanation of the relationship of work and family for women, whereas others are supportive of role accumulation theory. For the findings that a larger than expected proportion of women with managerial positions are not currently married, and as levels of commitment and preparation required for a job rise, there is an increase in the proportion of childless women and a decrease in the proportion with three or more children, a role conflict conceptualization provides a reasonable explanation. That is, according to role conflict theory, one way of dealing with the role strain experienced by those with a demanding job and career ambitions typical of managers and professionals is elimination of roles (Goode, 1960). The present study found support for this position in the case of managers but not

Table 9.3
Relationship of Job Satisfaction and Marital Status
for Women (percentages)

Level of Satisfaction	Married or Cohabiting	Widowed, Divorced, Separated	Never Married
Very dissatisfied	2.9	3.5	5.0
Dissatisfied somewhat	7.3	11.5	6.7
Satisfied somewhat	37.2	35.0	47.2
Very satisfied	52.6	50.0	41.1
Total	100.0	100.0	100.0
n	441	200	180

χ^2 (6, N = 820) = 12.9, p < .05.

professionals, possibly because most of the professional women were in traditionally female jobs (Gutek, 1985), which are regarded as less demanding than male-dominated professions. Women who are managers, however, are all in nontraditional as well as demanding jobs.

Whether marital status predisposes one to become a manager or managerial ambitions affect marital status was not addressed; however, based on a review of the literature, Nieva and Gutek (1981) concluded that the impact of family roles for women is to "reduce a woman's involvement in the labor force, lower her career commitment, steer her into a traditional career, and reduce her career attainment" (p. 44). Other findings, especially those related to job satisfaction and familial circumstances, provide support for a role accumulation explanation. This conceptualization is helpful in explaining why, in spite of much evidence indicating that role conflict is experienced by working women with family responsibilities, the lowest levels of job dissatisfaction were found among married or cohabiting women as opposed to those not married or currently living with a man, and lower levels of job satisfaction were found among the never married.

An alternative explanation to role accumulation is one of expectation level—that married women expect little and are satisfied with little from their jobs because their families are more important to them (see Feldberg & Glenn, 1979, for a fuller explanation of this point of view). These data do not support such an explanation, in that almost the same proportion of widowed, divorced, and separated women report being very satisfied with their jobs as married women. Single women and those not currently married report the most dissatisfaction. This finding is especially noteworthy in the never-married group because the effects of age were controlled in these analyses; younger workers tend to be less satisfied than older workers (see Quinn & Staines, 1979). Being single has an effect independent of age.

Although it does not dispute the adverse impact family obligations can have on women's careers, this research indicates that it is necessary to consider the positive aspects of multiple roles as well. The theory of role accumulation suggests a more positive and optimistic path for women—marriage, some children, and a career. The number of roles one occupies may be less important than the effort associated with the roles. As Gutek, Larwood, and Stromberg (1986) state, "the most satisfying life style may be one where a person can accumulate many new roles without expending great quantities of energy in any of them."

REFERENCES

Andrisiani, P. J. (1978). Job satisfaction among working women. *Signs: A Journal of Women in Culture and Society, 3,* 588-607.

Andrisiani, P. J., & Shapiro, M. B. (1978). Women's attitudes toward their jobs: Some longitudinal data on a national sample. *Personnel Psychology, 31,* 15-34.

Angrist, S. A., Lave, J. R., & Mickelsen, R. (1976). How working mothers manage: Socioeconomic differences in work, child care and household tasks. *Social Science Quarterly, 56,* 631-637.

Appelbaum, E. (1981). *Back to work: Determinants of women's successful re-entry.* Boston: Auburn House.

Beckman, L. J. (1978). The relative rewards and costs of parenthood and employment for employed women. *Psychology of Women Quarterly, 2,* 215-233.

Bryson, R., Bryson, J. B., & Johnson, M. F. (1978). Family size, satisfaction, and productivity in dual-career couples. *Psychology of Women Quarterly, 3,* 67-77.

Chacko, T. I. (1983). Job and life satisfactions: a causal analysis of their relationships. *Academy of Management Journal, 26,* 163-169.

Cooke, R. A., & Rousseau, D. M. (1984). Stress and strain from family roles and work-role expectations. *Journal of Applied Psychology, 69,* 252-260.

Crosby, F. J. (1982). *Relative deprivation and working women.* New York: Oxford University Press.

Dixon, W. J. (1981). *BMDP statistical software.* Berkeley: University of California Press.

Feldberg, R., & Glenn, E. (1979). Male and female: Job vs. gender models in the sociology of work. *Social Problems, 26,* 524-535.

Goode, W. J. (1960). A theory of role strain. *American Sociological Review, 25,* 483-496.

Gove, W. R. (1973). Marital status and mortality. *American Journal of Sociology, 29,* 45-65.

Gray, J. D. (1983). The married professional woman: An examination of her role conflicts and coping strategies. *Psychology of Women Quarterly, 7,* 235-243.

Gutek, B. A. (1978). Satisfaction guaranteed. *Social Policy, 9,* 56-60.

Gutek, B. A. (1985). *Sex and the workplace: Impact of sexual behavior and harassment on women, men and organizations.* San Francisco: Jossey-Bass.

Gutek, B. A., Larwood, L., & Stromberg, A. (1986). Women at work. In C. Cooper & I. Robertson (Eds.), *Review of industrial/organizational psychology.* Chichester, England: John Wiley.

Gutek, B. A., Nakamura, C. Y., & Nieva, V. F. (1981). The interdependence of work and family roles. *Journal of Occupational Behavior, 2,* 1-16.

Hall, D. T. (1972). A model of coping with role conflict: The role behavior of college-educated women. *Administrative Science Quarterly, 17,* 471-486.

Hall, D. T. (1975). Pressures from work, self and home in the life stages of married women. *Journal of Vocational Behavior, 6,* 121-132.

Hall, D. T., & Gordon, F. E. (1973). Career choices of married women: Effects on conflict, role behavior and satisfaction. *Journal of Applied Psychology, 58,* 42-48.

Hayes, W. L. (1981). *Statistics.* New York: Holt, Rinehart & Winston.

Heckman, N. A., Bryson, R., & Bryson, J. B. (1977). Problems of professional couples: A content analysis. *Journal of Marriage and the Family, 39,* 323-330.

Herman, J. B., & Gyllstrom, K. K. (1977). Working men and women: Inter- and intra-role conflict. *Psychology of Women Quarterly, 1,* 319-333.

Johnson, C. L., & Johnson, F. A. (1977). Attitudes toward parenting in dual-career families. *American Journal of Psychiatry, 134,* 391-395.

Keith, P. M., & Schafer, R. B. (1980). Role strain and depression in two job families. *Family Relations, 29,* 483-489.

LaRocco, J. M., House, J. S., & French, J. R. (1980). Social support, occupational stress, and health. *Journal of Health and Social Behavior, 21,* 202-218.

Laws, J. L. (1979). *The second X: Sex role and social role.* New York: Elsevier.

Lemkau, J. P., & Pottick, K. J. (in press). The declining satisfaction of white-collar women in sex-segregated and mixed-sex occupations. *Journal of Vocational Behavior.*

Mueller, C. W., & Campbell, B. G. (1977). Female occupational achievement and marital status: A research note. *Journal of Marriage and the Family, 39,* 587-593.

Near, J. P., Rice, R. W., & Hunt, R. G. (1980). The relationship between work and nonwork domains: A review of empirical research. *Academy of Management Review, 5,* 415-429.

Nieva, V. F., & Gutek, B. A. (1981). *Women and work.* New York: Praeger.

Pleck, J. H. (1977). The work-family role system. *Social Problems, 24,* 417-427.

Pleck, J. H., Staines, G. L., & Lang, L. (1980). Conflicts between work and family life. *Monthly Labor Review,* pp. 29-31.

Quinn, R., & Staines, G. L. (1979). *The 1977 quality of employment survey.* Ann Arbor: Institute for Social Research.

Rapoport, R., & Rapoport, R. N. (1971). Further considerations on the dual career family. *Human Relations, 24,* 519-533.

Rosow, I., & Rose, K. D. (1972). Divorce among doctors. *Journal of Marriage and the Family, 34,* 587-598.

Scarpello, V., & Campbell, J. P. (1983). Job satisfaction: Are all the parts there? *Personnel Psychology, 36,* 577-600.

Sieber, S. D. (1974). Toward a theory of role accumulation. *American Sociological Review, 39,* 567-578.

Smith, R. E. (1979). *Women in the labor force in 1990.* Washington, D.C.: The Urban Institute.

St. John-Parsons, D. (1978). Continuous dual-career families: A case study. *Psychology of Women Quarterly, 3,* 33-42.

Thoits, P. (1982). Problems in the study of social support. *Journal of Health and Social Behavior, 23,* 145-158.

Verbrugge, L. M. (1983). Multiple roles and physical health of women and men. *Journal of Health and Social Behavior, 24,* 16-30.

10

Working Toward a Theory of Women's Career Development

LAURIE LARWOOD and BARBARA A. GUTEK

Work in this book and elsewhere indicates the need for a theory of women's career development to consider several facets, such as career timing, not readily examined through common theories of men's career development. Some of the pieces of a tentative theory are suggested here.

Is there a need for a theory of women's career development? Several of the earlier selections in this book, most notably that of Diamond, have reviewed portions of the literature and concluded that there is such a need. Our own thinking is that need must be established by three factors: A theory must apply to a significant population; a theory must be useful to both research and practice; and there must be some reason for believing that the prior thinking cannot be conveniently stretched to encompass the particular population.

The significance of the population of working women is now beyond any dispute. In the United States, 53% of working-age women are in the work force, compared to 76% of men; working-age women are 43% of the overall work force. That figure is up from 30% in 1950, and the U.S. Department of Labor estimates that the largest growth segment of the labor force in the next two decades will continue to be women. The experience of other countries is similar. For example, in

West Germany the proportion of women in the work force rose from 37% in 1961 to 49% in 1980 (Hesse, 1984).

As important as the numbers of women working is the change in what they are doing. Once thought of as "pin money," to supplement household income, or to provide additional spending money, women's income is now relied upon by most two-earner families. In a surprisingly large proportion of cases, women are the sole bread-winners (Nieva, 1985).

The fact that women's careers are serious comes through in other ways. For the first time women constitute over half of university-level students. The courses they are enrolled in are increasingly career oriented. For example, by 1980 women were over 22% of those obtaining M.B.A. degrees and 34% of those enrolled in undergraduate business programs (National Center for Educational Statistics, 1980). Marriage is being delayed by some of these women, and families are smaller. Because careers are important, women with good positions or those launched on their careers are less likely to drop out of the work force for long periods when they have children (Blau & Ferber, 1985). Those having the appropriate credentials take their careers seriously, work hard, and, with a fair measure of luck, are increasingly succeeding despite the problems they face (O'Neill, 1985).

Do we currently have a theory of women's career development useful in research or practice? Even the briefest examination of the chapters in this book shows that we do not—at least not one that is generally accepted. Most of the researchers associated with this volume cite differing studies in making their points. The points themselves each deal with different aspects of women's career development. Although one might expect that the different aspects would tap into narrow parts of career development theories that might not overlap, some of these researchers felt the need to go well beyond career development theory. Thus Martin, Price, Bies, and Powers (Chapter 4) cited aspiration and deprivation theories, Boardman, Harrington, and Horowitz (Chapter 5) applied personality theory, and Zanna, Crosby, and Loewenstein (Chapter 3) used reference group theory.

There is a need to provide a synthesis between these and related work by other researchers. Ideally that synthesis will create a framework within which each of the present studies—as well as others dealing with career development—may be seen in perspective. Similarly the synthesis will offer a guide as to where information is currently lacking. We would hope that the work that has already been done, when it has been unified by such a theory, would offer practical help for understanding the current situation of women's career development as well.

WHY THEORIES OF MEN'S CAREERS DON'T FIT WOMEN

At one time it was believed that if women's careers were ever found to be important, the theories and research into men's careers would undoubtedly fit them. That thinking has been described by both Diamond (Chapter 2) and Larwood and Gattiker (Chapter 8). It is important to realize, however, that the modal pattern of men's careers is unlikely ever to provide a good fit for the modal pattern of women's careers. This is not to say that women's career achievements are likely to be any less than those of men or that some women do not fit the male model. Nonetheless, women on the whole face a somewhat different set of opportunities and problems than those seen by most men.

Many traditional male models propose that there are two early career stages (Hall, 1976; Hill & Miller, 1981; Schein, 1978). During the "education and exploration" phase (approximately ages 15 to 25) the individual learns job-related skills, maps career possibilities and goals, and "chooses" a career. Later in "identification and establishment" (25 to 40), young men identify with their careers and begin to move into them. Level, pay, and other objective measures of success are typically growing during the second phase. In a less well-accepted third stage, these indicators typically level out between the ages of 40 and 60 and career progress ceases, with the result of disappointment— "maintenance and stagnation"—leading to disengagement and retirement and a refocusing of interests outside the career (Bartolome & Evans, 1979; Hall, 1976; Kets de Vries, 1978; Korman, Wittig-Berman, & Lang, 1981; Shaw & Grubbs, 1981). A small number of the men avoid "maintenance and stagnation" either by continuing to grow successfully in their careers or by self-renewing change in direction (Driver, 1979; Larwood, 1984, pp. 485-486; Olson, 1977). For example, a person may reduce the amount of direct involvement with tasks and instead focus on developing young colleagues.

This model is, of course, greatly simplified. We know, for instance, that the first two phases are more rushed for those who merely see their careers as jobs than for those who take the time to obtain professional credentials. Similarly, we know that potential for avoiding stagnation is higher for those with substantial and appropriate education than for those without it (Rosenbaum, 1984). We also know that some people change careers and that this change can occur at any stage. There are nevertheless many elements specific to women's experience which the male model does not easily accommodate. Among these is the effect of basic social change in the treatment of and opportunities open to women. Men's opportunities and the expectations of them are seen as a constant. Depending on their upbringing and education, men can react to these in different ways. Nonetheless, essentially all men are expected (and expect) to engage in employment for a living. All are expected to aspire to upward mobility, and all are expected to be motivated by the promise of hierarchical success—at least until the promise loses credibility in the stagnation stage of their careers. In contrast, until the past two decades women were assumed to aspire to leaving their careers in favor of a family. Society socialized women toward this belief and structured rewards so as to encourage it. Thus firms discriminated openly against women in both selection and pay and universities discriminated in admissions (Larwood & Wood, 1977, pp. 3-28; Nieva & Gutek, 1981, pp. 54-81; Ratner, 1980). Women were prohibited by law in most states from accepting many jobs, including night jobs, bartending, mining, and jobs at firms with a concrete floor. Now both the beliefs and the structures designed to reinforce them are being largely swept away by social change. A satisfactory theory for women must be able to account not only for what is happening to young women today but what is happening to older women who were caught by the shift.

An equally obvious difficulty with applying theories intended for men's career development to women is the treatment of family life largely as an external irrelevancy. This is possible because it is assumed that men will continue to work after their marriage and after the birth of children, perhaps with greater urgency. The greatest burden imposed by marriage and children was assumed to be financial, but fatherhood was assumed to take relatively little time and emotional energy. Although increasingly recognized as a possibility, paternity leave, or a husband's leaving his job to take care of children, is still often viewed derisively (see Kauppinen-Toropainen,

Haavio-Mannila, & Kandolin, 1984). In contrast, homemaking was long seen as the archetypical career for women. Both employers and women knew as a certainty that women workers would take maternity leaves—and that they were unlikely to return to their jobs soon. Now, however, most women do return (see Fernandez, 1986, pp. 6-11, 107-115), if they even leave at all. The question of how such absences, their timing during the career, and their spacing affect the career is an important one that is all but alien to men's traditional career development.

There is an interesting paradox contained in the foregoing discussion. Although most men are described in part by the male career model, some are clearly missed. What happens to the man who does decide to throw caution to the wind, let his wife be the sole breadwinner, and take a paternity leave? What happens to the man who is untouched by promises of advancement, or who is touched at an inopportune time by social change wiping away the career he aspired to enter? Oddly, a broad model of women's career development may improve our knowledge of the nonconforming man. In effect, a good model of career development for women may be the more general model for both sexes.

DISTINGUISHING THE ELEMENTS OF A THEORY

If a comprehensive theory of women's career development is needed, what should the elements be? It seems to us that five concerns need to be added or given particular attention for women: career preparation, the opportunities available in the society, the influence of marriage, pregnancy and children, and timing and age. Despite giving special attention to these concerns, it should be recognized that we also feel that most of the problems and stages identified for men are important; these are interwoven with the elements emphasized below.

Career Preparation

Education and training have always been considered an important aspect of career development. The most usual ways to consider education have been that it was present or absent, professional or nonprofessional, or that it had reached a particular level. Those variables are important, but a more basic question remains: Was the woman (or man) prepared to engage in a career at all? A youngster who does not anticipate later being self-supporting is less likely than one who does to absorb vicarious socialization from watching the working world or to pay attention to her parents at dinner as they discuss their jobs. As a young adult she can afford to engage in college courses with no obvious practical application, and can afford the luxury of feeling that any subsequent jobs are temporary and thus need not lead anywhere. By this point she is unlikely to be able to see such opportunities as do exist for career development and will be able to retrain her way of thinking only with difficulty.

Opportunities Available

There is an American adage that "you make your own opportunities." The adage is true only in relative terms, however. Although opportunities may be nominally available (as, for instance, anyone can run for president), they are often realistically available only to those who have followed particular career paths providing appropriate preparation and acquiring appropriate experiences. Any theory of women's career development must add a dimension to this. Opportunities are also circumscribed by social pressures such as role norms and legal regulations. Until recently women were not allowed to obtain professional degrees in many universities; other schools discriminated in admissions standards. Similarly, firms such as AT&T maintained corporate policy that women could work only below particular levels and in a limited range of tasks. The U.S. military still does not allow women to obtain training in combat ships or aircraft. With limited opportunities, the motivation to obtain career preparation is necessarily diminished while dependence and the need for marriage as a source of financial support is increased. Subsequent to any increase in opportunity, it may take some time for recognition of the change to occur, and further time may be needed for women to obtain the preparation needed to take full advantage of the new situation.

Marriage

As was noted earlier, marriage has been viewed as neutral for men but one of the most damaging elements to the careers of women. The traditional Western family was viewed as that in which the husband supported a nonworking wife, and families with working wives were primarily confined to the lower middle and lower classes in which the additional income was required for a tolerable living standard. Other than in the latter groups, marriage was expected to interrupt the woman's career for an extended period of time—whether or not pregnancy followed. In point of fact, a large proportion of women rejoined the labor market following the death of their husbands or after divorce. By the time they returned, their skills were eroded and they could expect lower pay if they were previously well trained (Olson & Frieze, 1986; Bernard, 1971). Whether or not the woman expected continued employment, however, an employer might anticipate her leaving by offering only easy-entry positions with low training requirements. Although employers are now prohibited from discriminating on this basis, it still occurs; similarly, although the two-earner family is now normative, many families still prefer that the wife remain at home. A theory of women's career development must allow for varying alternatives.

Pregnancy and Children

As with marriage, the previous social norm held that women would interrupt their careers for pregnancy and would not return until the last child no longer needed care—if they returned at all. The mean period of interruption has been steadily declining. Most pregnancies and postnatal care now fall well within the average employer's requirements for a leave of absence. Still, a woman who is not prepared for a career, who sees little opportunity in it, or whose partner discourages it, may terminate her employment on becoming pregnant. In other words, a theory of career development should be "roomy" enough to consider both women who follow the traditional model and those who choose to have their children and get on with their careers.

Timing and Age

It has been said that it takes 20 years to reach middle management at General Motors. If true, it makes less sense for such a firm to hire aspiring managers at the age of 45 than at 25. A woman who enters the work force at middle age is more likely to find her career limited than a younger woman first entering it with identical credentials. Many women feel they are better advised to start their careers before leaving briefly to have children than to have the children first—although there is as yet no empirical research to show whether this belief is true. Older women who have remained consistently in the work force have a related problem. In determining who should advance or be given a particular assignment, the halo effect plays a large role. Without objective standards, employers judge future potential by past experience. Because older women were previously discriminated against, their past experience is likely to compare unfavorably with that of men of the same age and training who may be in higher-level and higher-paying positions. As a result, older women have a more difficult time obtaining a fresh evaluation of their performance and may move ahead more slowly than younger women. Timing and age should be considered in a woman's career theory (see Bernard, 1971) but are generally not considered in male-oriented theories because men are assumed to have been continually involved in the job market at a constant level of opportunity. (It is interesting that the traditional interruption in a man's career progress—a stint in military service— is often viewed as an opportunity to add career skills. In addition, men who have spent time in the military are often given preferential treatment through educational aid and hiring policies to compensate their contribution to society.)

PUTTING THE PIECES TOGETHER

How does the resulting theory look? One way in which to conceptualize it is to add the relatively simpler male model to the elements of women's career development. Career preparation most often occurs during the education and exploration phase. Examination and utilization of the opportunities available are most likely to take place in the first phase and in the second (identification and establishment) phase of the male model. Marriage and pregnancy are most likely to occur in the identification and establishment phase. The relationship can never produce a one-to-one correspondence, however, because of the timing and age problem. For a woman who delays her career by a decade or two with pregnancy, serious career preparation may have been similarly delayed (Bernard, 1971). Thus the resulting theory might better be seen as a network or tree of possible alternatives, each particular combination of which has a potentially different set of most likely outcomes.

Using the network concept, the most likely career paths to lead to hierarchical success for men and for women are identical. These are diagrammed below in italics.

The Situation Most Likely to Lead to Hierarchical Success

Career Preparation	Opportunities Available	After Marriage	After Pregnancy	Timing
yes	*yes*	*work*	*work*	*immediate*
no	no	no work	no work	delayed

In words, here an adolescent is prepared by those with whom she is in contact to anticipate a career, finds that the opportunities necessary for her career seem to be available, and embarks on it. Whether or not she marries, and whether or not she has children, she remains committed to working and returns as rapidly as possible. There are no timing delays, and thus she is launched in her career at the same age as a male would begin. Because of this sequence one might make roughly the same predictions for her career as for that of a man. She will have some difficulty being totally involved with both her career and her family (and may choose not to marry or not to have children). She is likely to peak and reach stagnation somewhere between age 40 and 60—although rare for anyone, she may alternatively continue toward the top in her profession or in a major organization. Two differences still divide men and women. Women will feel the tug of alternative possibilities such as concentrating on raising their children; if their peak occurs early enough, they might still do this while a man facing early career frustration may be less able to turn toward his family. A second difference is that despite regulations against it, women are still discriminated against; the opportunities that appear available may in reality be substantially tarnished, thus showing progress and making other possibilities appear more interesting.

The traditional woman can also be described using the same five components. She makes decisions exactly the opposite of the woman described above and views the opposite opportunity structure:

The Traditional Situation of Women

Career Preparation	Opportunities Available	After Marriage	After Pregnancy	Timing
yes	yes	work	work	immediate
no	*no*	*no work*	*no work*	*delayed*

In this second situation the adolescent does not anticipate a career. Because of her class background or because of continuing social restrictions, there are few interesting career possibilities available, and she prepares psychologically for being a housewife instead. If she holds a job at the time of marriage, it is easy entry/exit, requires little training, and pays little. She leaves the job after her marriage if finances allow, or after pregnancy for as long a period as economically possible. If this woman reenters the work force or develops a career, it will be delayed considerably; she will be older and will be disadvantaged by both her age and lack of prior job experience.

Women with poor or unfortunate timing may have any of several mixes. One example is shown below:

A Situation with Delayed Timing

Career Preparation	Opportunities Available	After Marriage	After Pregnancy	Timing
yes	*yes*	*work*	*work*	immediate
no	no	no work	no work	*delayed*

Here the adolescent has received the same tutorial on the importance of developing a career as in the first example. However, after preparing herself for the career she was delayed. This plausibly occurred to most women who were originally intent on careers and who are now over 50 years old. Some were unable to obtain professional training (other than in "women's fields"), and most found that they were unable to obtain a job using it. Women who obtained professional degrees during World War II, for example, were required by legislation to give up their jobs to servicemen who returned home, even when the women had also served in the military. By the 1960s, those women who stuck it out were launched in their careers; nonetheless, they were barely ahead of younger women and men and had years of experience in jobs having little responsibility and few opportunities for advancement. In view of their work record and of their age, they were (and are) seldom seen as having high potential. Further, because their jobs provided little responsibility and challenge or opportunity for advancement, many peaked early and thus found interests outside their careers or focused on interpersonal relationships at work rather than trying to advance from a job with little opportunity. Seen from an objective standard, their behavior was consistent with the former normative expectation that women were not interested in their careers and were not sufficiently good as to compete with men. As Kanter (1977) argued, their behavior is also consistent with their jobs.

DOES THE THEORY FIT THE RESEARCH?

The theoretical perspective just described should be understood as "bare bones." The links necessary to show exactly how one phase leads into another or to predict that timing lags will hinder career development in one situation but aid it in another have not yet been suggested. The research necessary to describe the pieces themselves is barely sufficient, let alone the dynamics of how the pieces of the theory interrelate to one another. We would hope that the dynamics are examined by later researchers.

Nonetheless, at this point the pieces should be sufficient to categorize the research presented in this book. One may not yet be able to apply the theory to predict the outcome of research results, but the theory should be compatible with them. If so, the pieces may already be useful in helping place that research into perspective and in suggesting where future research might most profitably be directed.

Several of our articles reflect the influence of career preparation either explicitly or indirectly. The Bronstein et al. chapter analyzing the *vitae* and recommendations of women and men for academic appointments examined preparation both directly and indirectly. Their findings indicate that there are few apparent sex differences. Nonetheless, the findings also suggest that timing may be important by allowing those who start earlier to obtain better academic credentials when "recycling" themselves back into the job market. Quite different results were found by Boardman et al. (Chapter 5) in their comparison of the personalities of women from economically disadvantaged backgrounds with those who were conventionally better prepared for success. The disadvantaged group was found to differ in personality and also to differ in its likelihood of citing a social network as being important. Presumably those who succeed despite an unlikely preparation background need a different climate in which to develop.

The influence of opportunities available in which to apply career preparation is most directly addressed by the Thomas study of the evaluation process in the Navy (Chapter 6). Her research showed clearly that those not having the opportunities considered most important for promotion—more often women than men—were shunted into less desirable promotions where future opportunities were also limited. Zanna et al.'s examination of reference groups (Chapter 3) found that women with male reference groups more often felt deprived and pessimistic but made more money than other groups. Although causality is uncertain, it appears that those with different reference groups made different assessments of the opportunities available to them. Martin et al. (Chapter 4) manipulated the apparent set of opportunities available to women and found that the opportunity set influenced both the level of satisfaction and the level of aspiration of some study participants in a complex manner. One interpretation of the Martin et al. results is that reaction to changes in opportunity level depends on prior career preparation and expectations.

The Zanna et al. research found that married but childless women were more likely to be the ones with a male reference group, whereas single women more frequently had a mixed-sex reference group. More direct evidence of the influence of marriage and children is provided by the Valdez and Gutek study of working women in Los Angeles (Chapter 9). A relatively large number of women in managerial positions were divorced or separated and had few (if any) children. On the other hand, levels of job dissatisfaction were lower among these who were married.

Several of the studies, such as Bronstein et al. and Thomas, touched on the importance of the sequencing of events. Timing was considered most prominently by Larwood and Gattiker in their examination of the career paths of younger and older women and men. Their results showed that the paths most useful to one group are not necessarily as useful to another. Thus it is not only what decisions are made and actions begun but when they occur that determines the outcome of the career development process.

Overall, the results of the studies included in this book generally fit the pieces of theory developed here. Nonetheless, they also illustrate how far such pieces have to travel before they become predictively useful. Each of the studies was more complex than the brief descriptions just given. No theory can be considered a complete success until those complexities are anticipated by future theoretical and empirical work. It seems assured that future research on career development cannot ignore the additional dimensions that research with women brings to the field, however, despite its added complexity.

REFERENCES

Bartolome, F., & Evans, P. A. L. (1979). Professional lives versus private lives—Shifting patterns of managerial commitment. *Organizational Dynamics*, 7(4), 3-29.

Bernard, J. (1971). *Women and the public interest: An essay on policy and protest.* Chicago: Aldine.

Blau, F. D., & Ferber, M. A. (1985). Women in the labor market: The last twenty years. In L. Larwood, A. H. Stromberg, & B. A. Gutek (Eds.), *Women and work* (Vol. 1, pp. 19-49). Beverly Hills, CA: Sage.

Driver, M. (1979). Career concepts and career management in organizations. In C. L. Cooper (Ed.), *Behavioral problems in organizations.* Englewood Cliffs, NJ: Prentice-Hall.

Fernandez, J. P. (1986). *Child care and corporate productivity.* Lexington, MA: D. C. Heath.

Hall, D. T. (1976). *Careers in organizations.* Santa Monica, CA: Goodyear.

Hesse, B. (1984). Women at work in the Federal Republic of Germany. In M. J. Davidson & C. L. Cooper (Eds.), *Women at work* (pp. 63-81). Chichester, England: John Wiley.

Hill, R. E., & Miller, E. L. (1981). Job change and the middle seasons of a man's life. *Academy of Management Journal, 24,* 114-127.

Kanter, R. M. (1977). *Men and women of the corporation.* New York: Basic Books.

Kauppinen-Toropainen, K., Haavio-Mannila, E., & Kandolin, I. (1984). In M. J. Davidson & C. L. Cooper (Eds.), *Women at work* (pp. 183-208). Chichester, England: John Wiley.

Kets de Vries, M. F. R. (1978). The midcareer conundrum. *Organizational Dynamics, 7*(2), 45-62.

Korman, A. K., Wittig-Berman, U., & Lang, D. (1981). Career success and personal failure: Alienation in professionals and managers. *Academy of Management Journal, 24,* 342-360.

Larwood, L. (1984). *Organizational behavior and management.* Boston: Kent.

Larwood, L., & Wood, M. M. (1977). *Women in management.* Lexington, MA: D. C. Heath.

National Center for Educational Statistics. (1980). *Earned degrees conferred in higher education.* Washington, DC: U.S. Government Printing Office.

Nieva, V. F. (1985). Work and family linkages. In L. Larwood, A. H. Stromberg, & B. A. Gutek (Eds.), *Women and work* (Vol. 1, pp. 162-190). Beverly Hills, CA: Sage.

Nieva, V. F., & Gutek, B. A. (1981). *Women and work: A psychological perspective.* New York: Praeger.

Olson, J. E., & Frieze, I. H. (1986). Income determinants for women in business. In A. H. Stromberg, L. Larwood, & B. A. Gutek (Eds.), *Women and work: An annual review* (Vol. 2). Beverly Hills, CA: Sage.

Olson, T. H. (1977). *Self-renewal and career development.* Paper presented at the annual meeting of the Western Academy of Management, Sun Valley, CA.

O'Neill, J. (1985). Role differentiation and the gender gap in wage rates. In L. Larwood, A. H. Stromberg, & B. A. Gutek (Eds.), *Women and work* (Vol. 1, pp. 19-49). Beverly Hills, CA: Sage.

Ratner, R. S. (1980). The policy and the problem: Overview of seven countries. In R. S. Ratner (Ed.), *Equal employment policy for women* (pp. 1-52). Philadelphia: Temple University Press.

Rosenbaum, J. E. (1984). *Career mobility in a corporate hierarchy.* New York: Academic Press.

Schein, E. H. (1978). *Career dynamics.* Reading, MA: Addison-Wesley.

Shaw, J. B., & Grubbs, L. L. (1981). The process of retiring: Organizational entry in reverse. *Academy of Management Review, 6,* 41-47.

Index

About the Contributors

Robert J. Bies is Assistant Professor of Organization Behavior at the Kellogg Graduate School of Business, Northwestern University. His research interests include the management of moral outrage, the use of justifications and apologies, fairness in communication, and the delivery of bad news in organizations. He received his Ph.D. in business administration (organizational behavior) from Stanford University.

Leora Black is a doctoral student in marriage and family therapy at the Department of Child Development and Family Studies, Purdue University. Her research focuses on adjustment to divorce.

Susan K. Boardman received her Ph.D. in social psychology from Columbia University and is currently working as Research Associate for the Center on Education and Employment at Teachers College, Columbia University. Her research interests involve achievement motivation, achievement-related conflicts, interpersonal conflict resolution, the psychology of gender differences, and the psychological, behavioral, and attitudinal antecedents of career success. Recent articles include "Neurotic Fear of Success, Fear of Failure, and Need-Achievement" (1983) and "Strategies for Career Success" (1984).

Phyllis Bronstein received her Ph.D. from Harvard in 1979. She is an assistant professor in the Department of Psychology at the University of Vermont. Her research interests include general socialization, women's professional advancement, and parent child interaction. Currently she is completing a book to be published by Wiley in 1987

entitled *Fatherhood Today: Men's Changing Role in the Family* and
is preparing another book to be published by the APA, *Teaching the
Psychology of People: Research for Gender and Sociocultural
Awareness.*

Faye Crosby is Professor of Psychology at Smith College. She is the
author of numerous articles on women and work and of the book
Relative Deprivation and Working Women (Oxford University Press,
1982). In 1987, Yale University Press will be publishing a book
Crosby is editing entitled *Spouse, Parent, Worker: On Gender and
Multiple Roles.*

Esther E. Diamond received her Ph.D. from Loyola University in
educational and psychological measurement in 1968. Her research
focuses on test development and related research—aptitude, interest,
and achievement tests; career development programs and materials;
and structured interviews, questionnaire development, and other
noncognitive assessment instruments. She is a Fellow in the American Psychological Association and recipient of the 1978 Distinguished Professional Service Award, American Personnel and Guidance Association. She is the editor, author, or coauthor of several
books and technical manuals and more than 45 book chapters and
journal articles in various areas related to psychological assessment.

Urs E. Gattiker, Ph.D., is Assistant Professor of Organizational
Behavior at The University of Lethbridge in Alberta, Canada. He
received his Ph.D. at Claremont Graduate School in organization and
management. Gattiker's areas of specialization and prior publication
include career development, technological change, computerization
and quality of work life, and management consulting. Gattiker is
currently on the editorial board of *Group & Organization Studies* and
writing a book, *Career Management: A Strategic Approach.*

Barbara A. Gutek is Professor of Psychology at The Claremont
Graduate School. She received her Ph.D. from the University of
Michigan in 1975, specializing in organizational psychology. She is
author, coauthor, or editor of six books, including *Women and Work:
A Psychological Perspective* (with Veronica F. Nieva, 1981), *Sex and
the Workplace: The Impact of Sexual Behavior and Harassment on
Women, Men, and Organizations* (1985), and *Women and Work: An
Annual Review* with Laurie Larwood and Ann H. Stromberg).

Charles C. Harrington is Professor of Anthropology and Education, Director of the Institute for Urban and Minority Education, and a Principal Investigator in the Institute for Education and the Economy at Teachers College, Columbia University. He is author of several books, including *Errors in Sex-Role Behavior* (1970), *The Learning of Political Behavior* (1970), and *Psychological Anthropology and Education* (1979). He is editor of *Readings on Equal Education*, an annual series whose most recent volume is *Race, Sex and National Origin: Public Attitudes of Desegregation*. He is currently completing a book describing the larger study from which his chapter is taken—*Paths to Success*. He received his Ph.D. from Harvard University in 1968. A psychological anthropologist, his work focuses on human development issues relating to social, ethnic, and gender stratification.

Sandra V. Horowitz is currently Evaluation Associate in the Office of Educational Assessment, New York City Board of Education. She is engaged in research on entitlement issues in intimate and work relationships. Other research interests include personality factors in health issues and the use of influence tactics for career success. She has a Ph.D. in social psychology from Columbia University.

Laurie Larwood is Professor and Head of the Department of Management at the University of Illinois at Chicago. She received her Ph.D. from Tulane University. Larwood has published extensively on women in management, career development, and consulting and is Editor of *Group and Organization Studies,* the *Journal of Management Case Studies,* as well as *Women and Work: An Annual Review* (with Barbara A. Gutek and Ann H. Stromberg). Among her books are *Women in Management* (with Marion Wood, 1977) and *Management and Organizational Behavior.*

George Loewenstein is Assistant Professor of Behavioral Science at the University of Chicago, Graduate School of Business. His current research interests include intertemporal decision making, expectation formation, and the psychology of preferences. He has a Ph.D. in economics from Yale University.

Joanne Martin is Associate Professor of Organizational Behavior and (by courtesy) Sociology at the Graduate School of Business, Stanford

University. Her research interests include economic inequality and distributive injustice, organizational cultures, and methodological departures from orthodoxy. She is currently writing a book tentatively titled, *Organizational Cultures: Homogeneity, Diversity, and Ambiguity*. She received her Ph.D. in social psychology from Harvard University.

Joyce L. Pfennig is a doctoral student at the University of Vermont. Her research interests include the relationship between attitudes and cognition.

Melanie E. Powers is a doctoral student in organizational behavior at the Graduate School of Business, Stanford University. Her research interests include factors in career differences between managerial men and women and the determinants of organizational structure. She received an S.M. in management from the Massachusetts Institute of Technology and an M.S. in statistics from Stanford University.

Raymond L. Price is currently employed by Hewlett-Packard and has worked in management and engineering and development. In these positions he has attempted to identify effective management and engineering practices and to use these methods to implement organization changes. Price received his Ph.D. in organizational behavior from the Graduate School of Business, Stanford University and his M.A. and B.S. from Brigham Young University.

Patricia J. Thomas is a research psychologist and branch head in Manpower and Personnel Laboratory of the Navy Personnel Research and Development Center. During the last 10 of her 22 years with the center, the primary focus of her research has been minorities and women in the Navy. Thomas is a member of the American Psychological Association and the Inter-University Seminar on Armed Forces and Society. She has been cited in *Who's Who Among American Women* and *Who's Who Among San Diego Women*.

Roberta L. Valdez is an organizational psychologist who received her Ph.D. from the Claremont Graduate School in 1986. Her research interests include flextime, multiple roles, and impacts of computers at work. She has been selected for inclusion in the 1986 edition of *Who's Who in American Colleges and Universities* and the 1986 *National*